REPRESENTING THE RESIDENTIAL REAL ESTATE CLIENT

Frank Taddeo, Jr.

Prentice-Hall
Englewood Cliffs, New Jersey

Prentice-Hall International, Inc., *London*
Prentice-Hall of Australia, Pty. Ltd., *Sydney*
Prentice-Hall Canada, Inc., *Toronto*
Prentice-Hall of India Private Ltd., *New Delhi*
Prentice-Hall of Japan, Inc., *Tokyo*
Prentice-Hall of Southeast Asia Pte. Ltd., *Singapore*
Editora Prentice-Hall do Brasil Ltda., *Rio de Janeiro*
Prentice-Hall Hispanoamericana, S.A., *Mexico*

© 1987 *by*

PRENTICE-HALL, INC.

Englewood Cliffs, N.J.

10 9 8 7 6 5 4 3 2 1

This publication is designed to provide accurate and
authoritative information in regard to the subject
matter covered. It is sold with the understanding
that the publisher is not engaged in rendering legal,
accounting, or other professional service. If legal
advice or other expert assistance is required, the
services of a competent professional person should
be sought.
*...From the Declaration of Principles jointly adopted by a
Committee of the American Bar Association and a Committee
of Publishers and Associations.*

Library of Congress Cataloging-in-Publication Data

Taddeo, Frank.
    Representing the residential real estate client / Frank Taddeo,
Jr.
        p. cm. Prentice-Hall law practice portfolio series)
    Bibliography: p.
    Includes index.
    ISBN 0-13-773763-7
    1. Vendors and purchasers—United States. I. Title. II. Series:
Prentice-Hall law practice portfolios.
KF665. T34 1987
346.7304'37—dc19
[347.306437]   **ISBN 0-13-773763-7**   87-24197
                                                        CIP

ABOUT THE AUTHOR: Frank Taddeo, Jr., is a practicing New York City lawyer specializing in residential and
commercial real estate law and litigation. Before entering private practice, he served as an attorney at RCA Corporation
and Warner Communications, Inc. He is a contributing author to *Administrative Law Treatise* (Matthew Bender: 1979),
coauthor of *The Legal Facts of Life* (E.P. Dutton: 1981)—a treatise on law for the layman done under the auspices of the
American Bar Association—and author of numerous articles on the law published by the *New York Law Journal* and other
periodicals. He also teaches real estate law at the Pratt Institute School for Continuing Education.

Printed in the United States of America

What This Portfolio Can Do for You

Some things never change. To own a new house, co-op, or condominium remains the American dream. Housing purchases and sales are still the only large-scale business transactions most Americans ever make. In an otherwise turbulent legal services market, they represent a constantly buoyant, often booming source of law business.

It is not a static business, however, and not necessarily an easy one. Buffeted by changes in legislation and case law, and by shifts in consumer habits and attitudes, residential real estate is a dynamic, evolving, frequently surprising challenge for attorneys. To practice it successfully, they must keep abreast of new developments, sift out time-worn information, and continually sharpen their negotiating techniques.

This portfolio is a practical, easily accessible, nuts-and-bolts source for modern residential real estate law. It is a reference tool that provides ready answers, stripped of pomp and legalese, when particular questions arise. More precisely:

This portfolio guides you through an entire real estate transaction, in sequence, step by step.

This portfolio provides you with an analysis of relevant state statutes and case law that bear directly on your transaction—law that makes practical points to integrate immediately into your game plan.

It suggests sound strategies and tactics for negotiating with opposite attorneys, bank lawyers, brokers, and even your own client, not necessarily to score adversarial points but to nurture the deal to a successful conclusion.

The portfolio includes tips on drafting, especially drafting associated with the major agreements such as the sales contract, broker's agreement, and amendments to both. It also offers advice on the several letters you will write during the transaction, letters that speak to the business relationships involved.

It includes checklists against which you can measure your activity, so your memory does not have to make all of the effort where details are involved.

It provides a series of warning posts and smart practice tips to help you avoid disputes that lead to litigation.

Some of the problems the book tackles:

How to communicate with your client and receive a reasonable fee for your work.

How to make the most of broker assistance by avoiding broker interference.

How to settle a contract of sale that disciplines both buyer and seller.

How to review mortgage papers, title reports, surveys and deeds, co-op and condominium offering plans, declarations, and bylaws.

How to compute closing costs and review a RESPA statement.

How to win tax advantages for your clients that may not be obvious.

The portfolio guides you through residential real estate transactions from start to finish, from the moment the client steps through your door to the closing—when the deed and keys are transferred from seller to buyer.

Chapter one focuses on cementing a professional relationship with your client. It shows you how to educate your client, in plain English, about the transaction ahead, and how to learn about the property at issue, the parties involved, and the other parameters of the deal. It also shows you exactly how to formulate a retainer agreement and set your fee, so that you will be paid on time and in full.

Chapter two takes a careful look at the property—the traditional house, a condominium, or a cooperative apartment. How are condos and co-ops organized? How binding are declarations, bylaws, and regulations, and how do their terms affect a purchase or sale? How do buyers finance a co-op purchase? These are just a few of the issues this chapter addresses.

Chapter three shows you how to deal with those individuals who play the game of real estate—brokers, inspectors, title people, and bank officials—and how they interact with attorneys during the course of a deal. It covers their legal statuses, their traditional manners, and their underlying motives in the deal.

Chapter four addresses the listing agreement between broker and seller, and a pseudo agreement between buyer and seller misnamed a "binder." What kind of listing agreements are there? When does a broker earn his or her commission? How should an attorney handle binders executed before the attorney becomes involved in the project.

Chapters five and six concentrate exclusively and thoroughly on the contract of sale, provision by provision, concept by concept, obligation by obligation. The chapters provide you with language variations, drafting techniques, and flash points of litigation, along with the law that has developed around those flash points. Chapter six includes discussions and samples of typical condo and co-op contracts, and how they compare with the traditional house agreement.

Chapter seven untangles the field of financing, focusing on the modern mortgage with all its permutations and combinations, and the disclosure requirements faced by lending institutions. It provides the practitioner with the working language to negotiate with those institutions and penetrate their often opaque requirements.

Chapter eight is devoted to the closing itself, the event that everyone's work prepares for—who attends, what exactly takes place, what calculations are made, how you must prepare, what documents are signed, what checks are cut, and what to avoid.

Chapter nine focuses on tax consequences of residential real estate transactions—what your clients must pay the IRS and when.

For easy reference, the portfolio ends with a table of the cases discussed, along with a selected bibliography of standard works that go into far greater depth on the subjects this portfolio treats.

Note, finally, that the portfolio contains no rigid division into a buyer's perspective and a seller's perspective. Rather it provides a total information picture for both sides so that a fair transaction will result. It treats the attorney not as an advocate solely for his client's position, but also as an advocate of the deal itself.

Dedication

To Michael R. Champi, with thanks.

Contents

REPRESENTING THE RESIDENTIAL REAL ESTATE CLIENT FLOW CHART

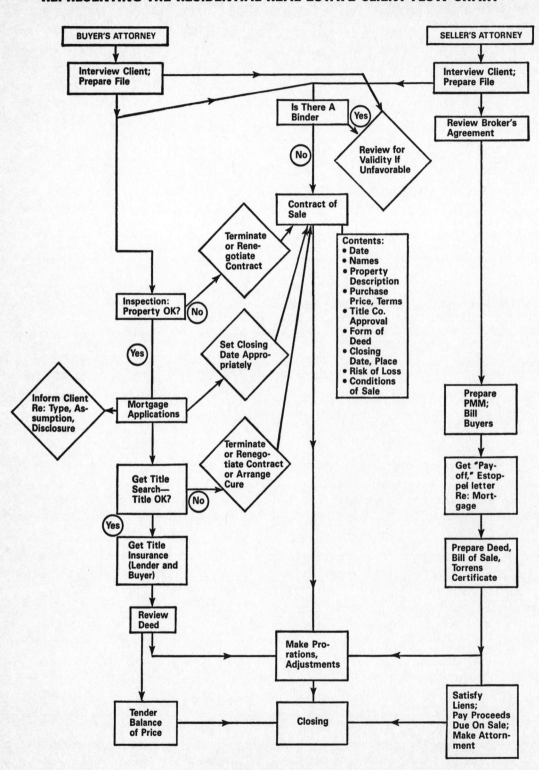

CLIENT INTERVIEW AND RECORDKEEPING

A business acquaintance of mine who dabbles in real estate never misses an opportunity to annoy me when we meet socially. Knowing of my real estate practice, he gleefully announces somewhere in our conversation that over the years he has bought and sold a number of houses and small apartment buildings successfully and never once used an attorney. "Why should I retain a lawyer," he asks. "and pay a stiff fee for advice I don't need."

To keep the discussion simple and short, I usually respond with the old seat-belts argument: thousands of people ignore the warning to "buckle up" and are never injured—hardly a commentary on the worth of the belts. He good-naturedly shrugs the argument off; and I do what I can to change the subject.

The repartee just described highlights a task you must perform in the initial interview with your would-be buyer or seller client. That he or she (or they) does appear in your office is at least some indication that the client thinks your services are valuable. But this is not conclusive evidence that the client will ultimately hire you, and, should the hire occur, that he or she will be cooperative and pay your bill. Consequently, you have to "sell" your services and yourself and to be sure that they are fully purchased.

You can accomplish this in three ways:

1. in plain English describe the steps of the transaction that lie ahead, tailoring the description to the sophistication of the client, and answer any questions the client may have;

2. gather information from the client through sharp questions of your own;

3. settle your fee arrangement clearly and conclusively in a written agreement.

SPEAKING IN PLAIN ENGLISH

When I say provide explanations in "plain English," that's what I mean—everyday language devoid of legalisms and polysyllabic words. Suppose, for example, a buyer-client wants to know how you plan to protect him in a contract of sale tendered by the seller's attorney, and this is the client's first real estate venture. Respond something like this:

> In this contract you will be agreeing to buy at a stated price subject to certain conditions. I will make sure that the contract specifies the purchase price, amount of cash down payment, method of financing, delivery date of property, right to inspect property, delivery of clear title, and survey. If certain items in the house are to be included as part of the sale—for example, carpeting or draperies—these need to be listed.

> As for the down payment, the contract must state that it is effective only if the seller can show satisfactory evidence of title and you qualify for a loan. The contract, among other things, must also provide for the return of your deposit if the seller does not comply with the terms of the agreement.

Maybe the client doesn't have the foggiest notion of how a mortgage works. Explain:

> A mortgage is a loan contract. A lender agrees to provide the money you need to buy your property. You in turn promise to repay the money based on terms set forth in the agreement. As federal law requires, the contract should state the amount of the loan, the annual percentage rate (which when computed includes the mortgage interest rate, the premium paid for insuring the mortgage, and certain "discount" points), the size of the payment, and the frequency of payments. Certain other charges that the lender will collect from you, such as penalties and prepayment privileges, along with any special conditions agreed on by the lender and you, must also be included.

> As the borrower, you pledge your home as security. It remains pledged until the loan is paid off. If you fail to meet the terms of the contract, the lender has the right to foreclose, that is, obtain possession of the property.

This is complex material, no doubt—but explained plain English.

If you are dealing with a seller, you will want to discuss the nature of broker listing agreements, and how commissions are negotiated. If there is no broker involved in the deal (the majority of the time there is), you will want to make sure your client—seller or buyer—understands the sequence of events, from binder to contract to inspections to mortgage application (assuming it is not an all-cash deal) to preclosing and closing, and where you fit into the sequence.

REPRESENTING THE BUYER

As for the sharp questions you, yourself, need to ask, base them on these checklists:

Checklist for Buyer as Client

A. General
  1. buyer personal data
     a. name (s)
     b. address (es)
     c. marital status
     d. dependants
     e. veteran or not
     f. financial condition
        (1) salaries
        (2) savings
        (3) investments
        (4) debts
  2. seller information
     a. name (s)
     b. address (es)
     c. attorney name, address, phone number
  3. broker information
     a. name
     b. address
     c. phone number (business & home)
  4. taking property as
     a. tenant in common
     b. joint tenant
     c. tenant by entirety

      d. as investment
      e. as residence
   5. time constraints
      a. lease expiring
      b. to sell current residence by certain date
      c. employment considerations
      d. planned closing date
   6. tax considerations

B. Buyer Actions Already Taken

   1. formal offers accepted
   2. documents signed
   3. mortgage research conducted
   4. notices given respecting home and work
   5. earnest money paid
      a. amount
      b. party holding
         (1) broker
         (2) seller
         (3) seller's attorney
   6. inspections done
      a. engineer
      b. termite
      c. title
      d. survey
      e. other
   7. moving arrangements made

Here are a few points to note about the above checklist:

First, you want to know about buyer's salaries and income to render an early bit of sound advice. ***PRACTICE TIP:*** *Advise your client that a buyer ordinarily should spend no more than two to two-and a-half times his or her total annual income for a home; and housing expenses should be limited to one week's pay out of each month's salary.* Of course, this is a general rule subject to all sorts of variables (a large family should spend less because it needs more money for food and other necessities than a single individual or childless couple). Nonetheless, it has validity; and if your buyer is reaching beyond the threshold, the banks are likely to refuse a mortgage, and even if a mortgage is acquired, the buyer may face serious financial woes.

You want to know if the buyer is a veteran because he or she is potentially eligible for VA financing and perhaps for preferential real estate tax rates.

Whether the new property will be used as a home office or business will tell you about possible tax deductions and the availability of depreciation.

As for buyer actions already taken, you must, obviously, pay immediate attention to documents already signed. You want to determine what concessions have been made and rights conceded; and if it is possible to modify, with the consent of the other side, any truly objectionable terms. When you represent the seller, you need not worry quite so much because, while you may be confronted with an already executed broker's agreement, you generally prepare the contract of sale, the key document in any real estate contract.

REPRESENTING THE SELLER

Checklist for Seller As Client

A. General
    1. names and addresses
        a. seller
        b. buyer
        c. buyer's attorney
        d. broker
        e. seller's bank
    2. present marital status
    3. past marital history
    4. time constraints
        a. closing date on new house to be purchased
        b. shifting value of target property
    5. mortgage on target property
        a. paid off or amount yet to be paid
        b. due on sale clause
        c. prepayment penalty
        d. assumption permitted or not
    6. incumbrances on house
        a. mechanic's lien or judgment lien
        b. taxes
        c. business loan
    7. tax questions
    8. financing seller supplying
    9. financial details
        a. monies due on new seller purchase deal
        b. points on buyer's mortgage
        c. broker's fee
        d. if bridge loan necessary

Why do you want to know the seller's marital history? There can be any number of reasons. One: It's not unheard of for an estranged husband or wife to attempt to sell a home despite a separation agreement or divorce decree that mandates a sale at a later time, or to try to keep all of the sale proceeds when they have already agreed or been ordered to share the proceeds or place them in trust.

You should ask about tax consequences because you want to know whether the target property has been partially or wholly used as income property or a home office (precluding nonrecognition of gain under Code Sec. 1034 unless there has been an "insulation" period). You also want to know if depreciation has been claimed and must be recaptured. Finally, suppose the seller is over age fifty-five. He or she is then permitted $125,000 in housing sale profits from income for tax purposes.

Just as the buyer's attorney must educate the buyer on the costs connected with the transaction, the seller's attorney must educate his or her client as to such costs and how they are paid. ***PRACTICE TIP:*** *Let the seller know that the usual custom is for the seller to pay for tax stamps or other charges involved in transferring a deed.* A common circumstance is for a lender to require the seller to pay one or more points on the buyer's mortgage (especially where a VA or FHA mortgage is involved, and the buyer's points are limited).

If a broker is involved in the deal, you need to know whether it is pursuant to an exclusive or nonexclusive listing, when the broker's fee will be earned, whether all brokers involved in the transaction are licensed, the respective roles played by the brokers and others in bringing about the sale, and whether the seller will pay the broker's commission separately at closing or pursuant to any other seller/broker arrangement.

Target Property Checklist (Buyer and Seller)

1. exact address
2. if resale
   a. one-family, two-family house
   b. condominium
      (1) unit number and description
      (2) condo name
      (3) percentage of common elements
      (4) monthly charges and assessments
      (5) other costs (for example, utilities)
   c. cooperative
      (1) in common, trust, corporate
      (2) corporation name
      (3) unit number and description
      (4) number of shares
      (5) monthly maintenance charge (rent)
   d. rental units (or place of business)
3. new construction

4. purchase price

   a. down payment ("earnest money")
   b. mortgage to acquire
   c. cash at closing
   d. seller financing available

5. taxes (amounts, due dates)

6. physical condition

7. insurance coverage

8. nature of area (flood, etc.)

9. zoning rules and regulations

10. personal property (included, excluded)

11. existing tenants

SETTING AND COLLECTING YOUR FEE

Naturally one of your first considerations as you take a real estate case must be setting and stating a fee for your work that will be accepted by the buyer or seller seeking your services. Inasmuch as most people are embarrassed to talk about money when they engage an attorney for legal service, it is wise for you to introduce the matter and settle it one way or another during your first interview with the prospective client, whether that interview is on the phone or in person.

PRACTICE TIP: Traditionally real estate lawyers use a thumbnail guideline for real estate transactions. The fee for the seller's attorney is often one percent (1%) of the sales price; for the buyer's attorney, one-half of one percent (½%). I don't know why this discrepancy developed—especially because in some states, New Jersey being a prominent example, the buyer's attorney has far more to do than the seller's.

Like most rules of thumb, this one must be considered in light of other considerations such as the attorney's expertise, the client's ability to pay, the nature of the deal itself, what is traditional or customary in the area, and fee guidelines that may be issued by state or local bar associations. As a businessperson, you must also be aware of the competition: Are there active legal clinics or discount law firms in your region, working on lower-than-traditional fee scales? And as a businessperson you must use common sense and quick wits to avoid money headaches.

What headaches? Herewith two of my own from the not-too-distant past:

EXAMPLE: On one occasion I represented the buyer of a condominium. At the beginning of the transaction, I quoted her a fee of one-half percent of the purchase price. The seller's lawyer was supposed to prepare the contract of sale; however he did nothing except mail me an incompletely filled out form agreement without including a copy of the deed or a standard schedule of added terms. So I had the unanticipated extra task of doing the seller's attorney's work, namely preparing a usable contract.

But that wasn't the worst of it. The buyer's son fancied himself something of a financier; he convinced his mother that he could broker her mortgage and received her go-ahead to try. To my repeated requests for an update on the progress of the mortgage, the son delivered an optimistic "any day now" message. He handled things so poorly, as it turned out, that I myself had to settle a bank loan for my client after untangling the mess her son created—even more unanticipated work, for which I received no compensation because I had quoted a flat fee.

PRACTICE TIP: What I learned from this experience was that it is wisest to enter into a retainer agreement with a client before the work commences and define very carefully the services to be included in the fee—making it clear in the agreement that a charge at the normal hourly rate will be assessed for extraordinary services.

Generally speaking, collecting a fee for real estate work is not as complex as it is in other branches of the law. Inasmuch as most property transactions involve the transfer of substantial monies, clients view payment to attorneys as simply one more check to change hands at the closing. To the buyer the payment is relatively insignificant when compared to what he transfers to the seller. To the seller, delighted at the monies he is receiving from the buyer, the payment is one he is usually happy to make. And the closing, practically and psychologically, is the perfect time for the counsel fee to be delivered—when the parties, bank a and title company are settling accounts and ending the transaction. *PRACTICE TIP: Unless the circumstances are extraordinary, insist on receiving payment at the closing, no later.*

Sometimes, however, collecting a fee can be quite unpleasant. Consider this example.

EXAMPLE: A young couple asked me to handle the purchase of their first house—a cape in a New York suburban area. I asked the usual questions and agreed to take the assignment. They wondered what my fee was; and I told them I would charge ½ percent as was my usual practice. They wondered if I could not do a little better on the fee, and I politely said that I could not, all things considered—the nature of the job ahead, my office overhead, my level of expertise and experience, and the like. If the legal fee was a problem, I suggested, they could contact one of the numerous legal clinics in their neighborhood and possibly locate an attorney who would agree to work for less. No, I had come "highly recommended" and so they wanted me.

After the first interview, I sent them a letter that, among other things, confirmed my charge and invited their comments on it, whatever they might be. Silence.

Several months later we attended the closing. Early on, I noticed that something was not quite right with my clients. They greeted me frostily, and seemed reluctant to talk. I asked if anything was the matter, and they said "no." It turned out that a traffic jam delayed the arrival of the seller's attorney (according to information supplied by his secretary); when I tried to make light of it and assure the couple that he would be along soon, they gave me a cold stare.

The closing proceeded routinely and quickly, and it came time for payment of my fee. The husband asked me how much it was, and I handed him a bill for the ½ percent. The wife gave it a disdainful look, and proceeded to tell me about a girlfriend who had just closed on a similar house and paid a far smaller legal fee. The husband said that it was only fair I lower mine. Allegedly, because I was so understanding about the delay of the seller's attorney, I had not been totally in their corner at the closing anyway. The attorney—me—demanded the fee "agreed on" (my clear fee letter, their silence in its face), and received it in full.

The painful lesson that came from this incident involves the age-old dilemma of proper communication. I should have detected possible trouble with the fee sooner, and been more careful in winning the couple's full acceptance of it. How? By making sure I had their signatures on my retainer letter, not just their silence in the face of my letter stating the fee. *PRACTICE TIP: Be sure to tender a final, formal bill to your client at the closing and include as charges, in addition to the base fee, any disbursements you made in the course of your representation, including travel, long-distance phone calls, telegrams or telexes, mail, and any extraordinary photocopy expenses.*

MAINTAINING THE FILES

A real estate transaction can generate a mountain of paperwork, most of which should be retained by buyer and seller for tax and other reasons. Here, to close the chapter, is a checklist of pertinent documents likely to pass your way prior to closing, along with a sample retainer agreement.

Checklist of Buyer and Seller Documents

1. ownership papers
   a. seller's old deed
   b. old certificate of title (if Torrens state)
   c. new deed (certificate of title) from seller to buyer
2. sales documents
   a. broker's listing agreement
   b. binder
   c. contract of sale (real property)
   d. contract of sale of personality (connected with property)
3. financial papers
   a. seller's mortgage or deed of trust

    b. seller's mortgage note

       (1) holder's name, address, telephone number
       (2) holder's attorney identification

    c. seller's mortgage satisfaction letter
    d. mortgagee's consent to buyer's assumption of seller mortgage (if assumable)
    e. buyer's mortgage application and associated bank papers
    f. buyer's mortgage

4. title related papers

    a. seller's old title report and survey
    b. buyer's new title report and survey
    c. affidavits supplementing chain of title (for example, regarding heirship, intestacy, liens)
    d. certificate of occupancy (indicating property complies with public health and building codes)
    e. other certificates and permits

5. tenant documents

    a. rent rolls
    b. leases
    c. service contracts
    d. payroll schedules

6. insurance

    a. seller's homeowner's policy
    b. seller assignment form naming buyer assignee (if assignment part of deal)
    c. buyer's newly purchased policy

7. inspection reports

    a. engineer's
    b. insect infestation
    c. other

8. fuel and utility bills

9. if condo

    a. offering plan
    b. financial statement and budget
    c. declaration, bylaws, rules and regulations

10. if co-op

    a. prospectus ("red herring")
    b. certificate of incorporation
    c. proprietary lease
    d. stock certificates

RETAINER AGREEMENT

Date:_____, 19_____

Dear_____:

   This letter confirms the agreement reached at my office/on the telephone on_____, 19_____.

You wish to retain me as your attorney for the purchase/sale of property located at_____ in the City of_____ and County of_____.

   The property is described as follows:_____

   The sale also includes personal property as follows:

_____.

   A closing has been tentatively scheduled for_____, 19_____.

   I agree to carry out the following tasks (and others reasonably related thereto):

[   ] Assisting with contract negotiation

[   ] Drafting a contract of sale/broker's agreement/binder

[   ] Assisting with financing and interpreting financing-related documents

[   ] Ordering/reviewing title insurance/engineer's inspection/termite inspection report

[   ] Drafting a purchase-money mortgage

[   ] Preparing for the closing (document assembly and review, liaison with title company, broker, financial institution, opposing counsel)

[   ] Attending the closing

[   ] Advising on the tax ramifications of the transaction. We have agreed that my fee for these tasks will be:

[   ] $_____ per hour, plus costs and disbursements, to be billed monthly

[   ] A flat fee of $_____, plus costs and disbursements, payable at the closing or on _____, 19_____ whichever is earlier

[   ] A flat fee of _____% of the sale price of the property, plus costs and disbursements, payable at the closing or on _____, 19_____, whichever is earlier.

   We have agreed that these fees include only those services up to and including closing of the transaction, and any follow-up duties associated with those services. If the transaction does not close for any reason, for example, if the buyer cannot get financing, or if the seller sells the property to another buyer instead, my fees will be as follows:_____.

   It is understood that any litigation arising from this transaction is not covered by this agreement. If you want me to represent you in such litigation, we must negotiate another retainer agreement.

We have agreed that other members of my firm may work on this matter if I am unavailable.

This letter contains all the terms of the agreement under which I will represent you. Any amendments to the agreement must be in writing and signed by both of us to be binding.

Enclosed are two copies of this letter. Please sign both and return one to me for my files. Very truly yours, (Signature)

THE PROPERTY

A housing transaction is different from other sales transactions because it involves property, one of the nation's great natural resources. Property is a place, not a product, one with legal and business history, a legacy—and an ongoing future. The transaction you handle is a benchmark in that future.

Here is a review of a few basic concepts. Your task as a real estate attorney is to render advice on that bundle of rights associated with real property—the estate in rights we call "real estate." A good working definition of "real property" is: the earth's surface extending downward to the center of the earth and upward into space—including all things permanently attached to it by nature or man, and including all interests, benefits, land rights associated with the ownership of real estate.

The real estate rights associated with real property include: ownership, possession, control, enjoyment, and exclusion; and the rights to will, mortgage, encumber, cultivate, explore, lease, license, share, trade, or exchange.

What types of residential real estate will you encounter? There are basically three kinds—house, condominium ("condo"), and cooperative ("co-op").

BUYING A HOUSE

Little need be said about a house except that it is the most common type of real property we know in America. Whether it involves a Cape Cod colonial, California bungalow, Dutch colonial, Tudor, French provincial, contemporary, or whatever, house ownership is fee simple ownership of the basic structure itself (the "house"), the sky above, and the mud below. The owner pays taxes on the building and land; usually holds title subject to a mortgage; and holds a witnessed and notarized deed to the property, recorded with a county recorder.

To transfer the real estate, you transfer the deed.

REPRESENTING THE CONDOMINIUM BUYER

Like the house, the condo entails ownership of real property: *LeFebvre v. Ostendorf*, 275 N.W.2d 154 (Wis.App. 1979). Unlike it, the condo involves fee simple ownership of an individual unit in a multi-unit project. Said one court:

> The basis of the concept is the theory that as a parcel of real estate it may be subdivided into contiguous lots; likewise, the area above the land may be subdivided into a number of 3-dimensional air spaces, each susceptible of being separately conveyed. *United Masonry Inc. v. Jefferson Mews, Inc.*, 237 S.E.2d 171 (Va. 1977).

A condo owner owns his unit—a standard, apartment-type living space or "town house" that resembles a conventional row house—and an undivided interest in the project's common elements, which he holds as a tenant in common with all of the other unit owners in the project: *Ventura v. Hunter Barrett & Co.*, 552 S.W.2d 918 (Tex.Civ.App. 1977).

Common elements include the land, foundation, elevators, main walls, yards, roof, gardens, parking areas, recreational facilities, corridors and lobbies, and installations for service (power, light, gas, hot and cold water, heating, refrigeration, incineration). An owner can alter or decorate the inside of his unit in any way he chooses, because he holds exclusive title to it. He cannot alter the exterior of the unit or common property. Only the representatives of the condo project have the latter right.

In one dispute an owner clashed with a condo association over a storm door attached with screws to the entry way of his unit. The court held that the owner's addition of the door was not an "addition or alteration of the exterior" within the meaning of the condo by law prohibition against adding to or otherwise altering the exterior: *Board of Managers of a Part of Peppertree Square No.1 v. Ricketts*, 701 S.W.2d 767 (Mo.App. 1985).

While common-law condos do exist, most are creatures of statute and as such are subject to the control and regulation of the legislature.

Under such state regulation, developers must file an instrument known as a "declaration"—a detailed plan of both organization and ownership. It usually includes the name of the condo, a description of the condo parcel, a legal description of each unit, the city and county in which the condo is located, and the location of the common areas. Most state statutes also require it to express the proportionate, undivided interest in the common areas pertaining to each unit.

There are two ways of determining the proportion fraction. One: the numerator is the unit's fair market value, the denominator is the fair market value of all the units as of the declarative date. Two: the numerator is the individual floor area, the denominator the aggregate floor area of all the units on the date of the declaration.

The declaration frequently contains the conditions, covenants, and restrictions all owners and other residents must honor: the condo's bylaws and "house rules." As one court put it, by laws represent a form of "private lawmaking" by the owners as a group. Owners agree to subordinate traditional, individual ownership rights and privileges for the good of the project as a whole: *Ryan v. Baptists*, 565 S.W.2d 196 (Mo.App. 1978). House rules deal with everyday conduct such as parking, trash disposal, and the use of the pool or other recreational facilities: *Dulaney Towers Maintenance Corp. v. O'Brey*, 418 A.2d 1233 (Mo.App. 1980).

EXAMPLE: Long ago, I reviewed a prospectus and declaration for a Florida condominium for an elderly couple about to retire. Drafted in close conformity with the Florida Condominium Act (FS 718.100-718.500), the prospectus indicated that the condo was a bona fide offering from a reputable developer. However, I noticed one problem with the prospectus.

According to FS 718.104 (4) (e), if construction of a condo is not substantially complete, there must be a prospectus statement to that effect. If it is substantially complete, the developer must include a certificate by an authorized Florida surveyor certifying substantial completeness and hence the accuracy of the location and dimensions of each part of the condo project described in the project.

The papers I reviewed had neither the requisite statement nor the surveyor's certificate.

As for the declaration, one paragraph concerned me. Typically developers share common expenses pro rata for unsold units. Here the developer announced that he would not, although the paragraph did set a ceiling on purchaser expenses. ***PRACTICE TIP:*** *With respect to any developer's estimates as to amount of common expenses to be paid, tell your client to count on paying twenty-five percent more.*

Early in a condo project's history—either at a predetermined date or after a certain number of units have been sold—the developer turns over the project's management to a board of directors (or managers) chosen by vote of the unit owners. The owners then adopt bylaws under the board's direction; the board makes the house rules.

While the board's rules and its administration of them must be reasonable (*Papalexiou v. Tower West Condominium*, 401A.2d 280 (N.J.Super. 1979)), the board itself has considerable power and latitude in running the project. For instance, if a unit owner ignores a bylaw restriction, the board can enforce it by injunction, *LeFebvre v. Osterndorf, supra*. However, the board itself cannot go beyond the bylaws and act *ultra vires* even if supported by a majority of homeowners.

In an Arizona dispute, the court held that nothing in the condo laws authorized a council of co-owners, although supported by a majority vote, to take part of the condo's common elements for the construction of additions to the basement and second floor. The taking of the property of other individual unit owners could only be given by statute, held the court; the relevant statute did not afford the council that right: *Makeever v. Lyle*, 609 P2d 1084 (Ariz.App. 1980).

Generally speaking, whenever a controversy arises over a unit owner's rights, the courts review the state statute covering the condo project; the condo declaration, bylaws, and rules, and attempt to reconcile all four for a solution. *Dulaney Towers Maintenance Corp. v. O'Brey*, supra.

Unless the declaration or bylaws forbid it, owners can sell or lease their units to anyone without restriction. With the same caveat, owners may mortgage their units. Because condo ownership qualifies as an interest in real property, banks and insurance companies freely extend mortgage loans to condo owners as they do to the owners of houses. Both classes of owners become subject to personal liability on the bond or note; neither ownership interest can be affected by the mortgage defaults of neighbors.

As for taxes, each condo unit is separately assessed for real estate tax purposes. The owner pays taxes directly to the town, county, or other government body involved. The owner pays his share of expenses for the operation, maintenance, repair, and replacement of the condo's common elements. In fact, many state statutes give the condo a lien on the unit of an owner who has failed to pay his share of common charges—a lien that is prior to all liens except first mortgage liens and real estate taxes. The condo can foreclose on a unit lien in the same manner in which a bank can foreclose on a mortgage lien.

Practically speaking, what happens when an owner defaults on paying assessments? The condominium can't use a summary proceeding to dispossess the owner, because there is no landlord-tenant relationship. It can bring a breach of contract action in search of damages; or, if appropriate, seek an injunction—not very satisfactory remedies.

Condo owners, like house owners, can deduct mortgage interest (their proportionate share of the project's) and real estate taxes for income tax purposes. They are personally liable for the project's bills and for tort claims against the project. While the project generally carries an insurance policy naming owners as insureds in proportion to their interests in the common elements, each owner can protect household and personal effects only by his own insurance.

The condo association (that is, a majority of the unit owners) frequently has a right under the bylaws to disapprove transfers by owners to would-be buyers. At least one California court has held that the association, in exercising its right to approve or disapprove, must act reasonably, in a fair and nondiscriminatory manner, withholding approval only for a reason rationally related to the protection, preservation, and proper operation of the property: *Laguna Royale Owners Ass'n v. Darger*, 174 Cal.Rptr. 136 (Cal.App. 1981). Disapproval on the basis of age is not *per se* unreasonable if there is no age restriction in the condo documents: *Ritchey v. Villa Nueve Condominium Ass'n*, 146 Ca.Rptr. 695 (Cal.App. 1978).

PRACTICE TIP: *Advise a buyer client against purchasing a condo that would be difficult to resell because of the narrow pool of buyers dictated by a restrictive declaration or bylaws.*

Checklist representing the condo buyer:

- Check your state's condominium statute to determine whether the condo project was validly created (meets the statute's minimum requirements). In states such as Minnesota, Missouri, Nebraska, or Pennsylvania, you'll be looking at the ABA's Uniform Condominium Act. In others, you'll deal with the state's individual statute.

- Review the declaration, bylaws, and regulations, paying particular attention to whether:

  •• the condo has a right of first refusal to buy the unit in question. If so, the owner must give proper notice of intention to sell.

  •• the buyer is required to execute a power of attorney to the board of directors or managers to acquire any unit the owner wants to sell, in the board's name on behalf of all the unit owners.

- Review any existing mortgage; if your client plans to assume a mortgage, research real estate tax assessments on the unit. Find out the percentage of common charges your client, the buyer, will have to pay.

- Contact a title insurance company; have it examine and insure title on the unit being purchased, and insure the valid creation of the condominium.

REPRESENTING THE CO-OP BUYER

A condo buyer's primary needs are psychological (to own his own home) and practical (to choose his own neighbors)—home ownership in what is generally an urban environment. In buying a unit, the buyer creates an asset for himself, an equity that may be devised, alienated, or borrowed against.

The co-op buyer has similar aims. The cooperative, like the condominium, involves living in an individual unit in a multiple dwelling, sharing common areas. Unlike the condominium, however, the cooperative can take on various legal forms, some quite different from the condominium. For instance, the California tenancy in common co-op is organized so that the occupants own the entire premises as tenants in common; the trust co-op, popular in Chicago, has a business trust acquire and manage the property that becomes the cooperative.

The most common co-op form, popular in states such as New York, is the corporate form. Here the tenants own shares of stock in a corporation holding title to the real property of the co-op complex. They hold a "proprietary" lease solely by virtue of that stock ownership, entering into a relationship not unlike a partnership, although expressed in a corporate form: *Penthouse Properties v. 1158 Fifth Avenue,* 11 N.Y.S.2d 417 (1939).

They own personal property, the shares of stock being choses in action; the corporation has title to the land. Actually, the stockholders have so many of the rights and obligations peculiar to fee ownership that their status, for all practical purposes, is indistinguishable from that of house and condo fee owners: *Silverman v. Alcoa Plaza Assoc.,* 323 N.Y.S.2d 37 (1971).

Co-op corporations are business corporations pure and simple, formed by the filing of a certificate of incorporation. The certificate includes the usual "purposes and powers" provisions and one unique to co-ops, providing for proprietary leases to the apartments in the building. The lease is a contract for the use of a given apartment, and may be short- or long-term. The lease is called "proprietary" because it recognizes that stock ownership is present. However, it is not an ownership document as such.

Tenant-shareholders have broad rights to use and alter the leased premises that tenants of rental properties do not enjoy. They can:

- amend the lease by shareholder vote
- remove objectionable tenants by vote
- approve or disapprove sublets or transfers of co-op interests, again by vote
- dissolve or continue a co-op venture indefinitely
- pay "floating" maintenance charges rather than fixed rent.

The corporation's affairs are governed by a board of directors elected by the tenant shareholders. Like the condo board, the board administers bylaws, house rules, and regulations shareholders must obey. Usually these bylaws, and rules, (for the proprietary lease itself) prohibit assignment or subletting without prior board approval.

So long as the board doesn't violate federal or state antidiscrimination laws, it can turn down an assignment or sublet request arbitrarily. In fact, it need not even give a reason for its denial.

EXAMPLE: By way of illustration of the relationship between a co-op board and co-op tenants: In one of my cases I represented the owners of an exclusive co-op they wanted to renovate. They hired a contractor who proceeded to perform the renovation but who refused to pay a subcontractor on the job because of a private dispute.

Subcontractor brought an action against the contractor and the co-op corporation operating the apartment building, and in addition slapped a mechanics lien on the building for the amount of the claim. The co-op board, citing a co-op bylaw for authority threatened to evict my clients if they did not discharge the lien within twenty days, which they did by posting a bond for that amount. At the closing of a co-op sale, a co-op corporation may seek from the incoming buyer monies to be held in escrow to cover various unenumerated actual and potential expenses.

PRACTICE TIP: Question these expenses sharply and strongly object to any requested escrow payment earmarked for the discharge of possible mechanic's liens.

What about the co-op owner's tax position? Section 216 of the Internal Revenue Code gives each tenant-shareholder a deduction of this share of the co-op corporation's real estate taxes and mortgage interest, if:

- the corporation has only one class of stock
- each shareholder is entitled to occupy an apartment for dwelling purposes
- at least eighty percent of the corporation's gross income is derived from the tenant-shareholders
- unless the corporation is partially or completely liquidated, the shareholders receive distributions only out of the corporation's earnings and profits.

An early step in representing a co-op buyer is to examine the co-op's certificate of incorporation and bylaws to make sure the corporation was validly incorporated. Another early task is to determine whether the IRS requirements have been met. *PRACTICE TIP: Check the eighty-percent qualification by reviewing the corporation's latest balance sheet and income expense statement.*

Now let's look more closely at the purchase itself. The buyer gets two legal grants for his money: an assignment of shares of the corporation's stock allocated to the unit being bought (usually based on the unit's rental value); and the proprietary lease to that unit.

The lease obliges the new tenant to pay his share of the corporation's property expenses in the form of rent. The corporation has all the remedies of a landlord to collect rent—including the right to a summary proceeding. It has a lien on the tenant's shares to secure the rent obligation.

How do co-op buyers finance purchases? A bank mortgage is one way, certainly. If the buyer qualifies, all he has to do is pledge his stock and lease as security. As a rule, banks treat co-op loans as personal loans and don't require formal appraisal of the values of the shares and lease; they're more concerned about the buyer-borrower's credit. Therefore, the buyer subjects himself to personal liability on the note accompanying the loan.

Before making the loan, the bank will want tax and judgment searches against the current owner of the shares and lease. It may also require title insurance for the buyer; if it doesn't, you should examine the building's title insurance and make sure it is in order. If the building policy is not recent, or if the corporation's indebtedness has not been refinanced, you should acquire title insurance protection for your buyer.

Here is something to keep in mind about newly formed co-op complexes.

Many state laws forbid the offer of real estate interests unless the offering party files a written statement (or prospectus) containing all of the material facts of the offering. Usually these laws apply to public offerings, not sales of single units (even if the owner advertises the sale).

Co-ops and condos fall under these laws. The prospectus of a validly filed public co-op offering—more popularly known as a "red herring"—will carry a legend on its cover stating that it has been accepted for filing. If you encounter no prospectus, or one not validly filed, the offering is illegal and you must advise your buyer to buy elsewhere.

By way of review and summary, here is a co-op checklist most useful when representing a buyer:

- Check the co-op offering plan (red herring), and certificate of incorporation to make sure the project was validly incorporated.

- Review proprietary lease, bylaws, house rules for living restrictions, paying particular attention to sublet and assignment rights.

- Check most recent corporate financial statement and determine pro-rata deduction for mortgage interest and real estate taxes (assuming that the eighty-percent qualification is met).

- Determine the unit's monthly maintenance charge and any changes contemplated by the co-op board likely to impact on that charge in the near future.

- Retain a title company to perform tax and judgment searches against the seller of the unit. Have the company also conduct a UCC search against the seller's co-op stock (creditors and banks, for example, file UCC statements to protect loans they issue for the purchase of personal property—like co-op stock).

3

THE PLAYERS

What makes practicing real estate law so fascinating is the fact that no transactions are exactly alike. The related law remains pretty much the same. The method of practice follows prescribed lines. The level of responsibility a lawyer takes on is not all that different from that associated with other legal practice. Yet, what is unique—distinct—is that real estate constantly yields surprises—new wrinkles on old themes, sometimes not so pleasant, but rarely boring.

Why this is so at least in part is because of the players involved, a shifting cast of characters performing in a relatively short time frame, seemingly toward the same goal, but not always.

Who are these players and what scripts do they follow?

21

DEALING WITH THE BROKER

The broker may be the most interesting player of all. The reason is that his or her work is complex and fraught with seeming contradictions.

In the normal deal, a broker nominally represents the seller, while in fact spending most of his time cultivating the buyer. He is the catalyst in the buyer-to-seller equation, convincing the buyer that the seller is sitting in a buyer's dream home, and that the dream could become a reality with a few strokes of the pen. Once the buyer agrees, the broker nurtures the deal through the contract, mortgage, and closing stages, sparring with attorneys, bank officials, title personnel, inspectors, and other brokers, as well as with the principals themselves. Salesperson, psychologist, teacher, diplomat; the broker has one singular objective: to achieve a closing and collect what is often a substantial fee. For in the typical transaction, only at closing does the broker receive his or her commission.

More specifically, brokers provide (or should provide) two specific services—advice and negotiating assistance. The advice service has three dimensions: (a) helping the consumer understand what is indeed a complex transaction—purchase and sale of real estate , (b) clarifying the legal status of the various actors in the transaction, so the consumer can base his or her decisions on accurate knowledge of the actors' responsibilities and interests, and (c) providing counsel about the purchase or sale of the particular home, including information about the advantages and disadvantages of the home and overall deal.

That brokers provide critical negotiating help in the usual deal, there can be no doubt. A consumer survey of the real estate industry done a few years ago under the auspices of the Federal Trade Commission, for example, made findings in this regard that even surprised the Commission. The survey discovered that seventy-eight percent of sellers and sixty-six percent of buyers questioned believed that their brokers were "representing" them in negotiating the contract price, and admitted that they were relying heavily on "their" broker's advice during all phases of the transaction.

The survey further discovered that both sellers and buyers generally tell their brokers the price beyond which they will not go in the deal; a surprising eighty-three percent of the buyers surveyed agreed that they "felt that whatever ['they'] told ['their'] agent about how high ['they were'] willing to go for the house would remain confidential." See Federal Trade Commission Staff Reports, The Residential Real Estate Brokerage Industry, Los Angeles Regional Office Staff Report: Volumes I and II and the Butters Report, December, 1983, p.78.

It is certainly an understatement to say that brokers take center stage in negotiations, that there is a potential conflict of interest in how they conduct business, and that you as a real estate attorney must sharply monitor their activity.

Here is a checklist of the types of brokers who work in real estate:

- alternative broker: one who advertises or publicly offers commission rates or services significantly different from the prevailing rates or services in the community. The terms "discount broker" and "flat-fee broker" refer to types of alternative brokers;

- broker: a licensed real estate practitioner; the more senior of the categories of real estate licenses (the other being "salesperson"), empowered by the state to handle real estate transactions;

- listing broker: the broker who has a listing agreement with the seller;

- Realtor (always capitalized): the trademark name for a broker-member of the National Association of Realtors;

- salesperson: a licensed real estate practitioner subordinate to broker; the more junior of the two categories of real estate licensees, handling many aspects of a real estate transaction not reserved for brokers only, and who must work for a licensed broker;

- selling broker: the broker who works with the buyer in the purchase of a home listed by another broker; also called a "cooperating broker";

- traditional broker: one who follows the prevailing mode of brokerage practice in the community, including prevailing commission rates (as distinguished from an alternative broker).

The principal trade association in the real estate brokerage business is the National Association of Realtors ("NAR"). With its fifty affiliated state associations and some 1,800 affiliated local Boards of Realtors, it is the largest trade association in the nation, and represents an overwhelming majority of all active brokers and salespersons. It licenses the trademark term "Realtor", operates approximately ninety-five percent of all the nation's multiple listing services, and performs a wide range of educational, political, and public relations functions. It also enforces a code of ethics and broker regulations.

What legal status does a broker hold? It is pretty much the same in every state. In Kansas, for instance, he or she is considered an agent who, for a fee, carries on negotiations on behalf of a principal, an intermediary between the principal and third persons on transacting business relative to the sale or purchase of contract rights or property. *Henderson v. Hassur,* 225 Kan.678, 594 P. 2d 650 (1979).

New Jersey courts define a broker as a person, firm, or corporation who, for valuable consideration, solicits for prospective buyers or assists in procuring products or negotiating or closing a transaction that results in the sale of real estate: *Baron & Co. v. Bank of N.J.*, 504 F.Supp. 1199 (D.N.J. 1981).

In a nutshell, a broker is an agent who works for a principal, most often the seller, for a fee pursuant to a contract of employment with that principal (*Munjal v. Baird & Warner, Inc.*, 485 N.E.2d 855 (Ill.App. 1985)—a special agent limited to showing property and finding a purchaser. He has no right or authority to consummate a contract on behalf of his principal: *UTL Corp. v. Marcys*, 589 S.W.2d 782 (Tex.Civ.App. 1979).

This agent/principal relationship is a fiduciary one, one requiring a high degree of honesty and trust between the parties: *Miller v. Iowa State Real Estate Commission*, 274 N.W.2d 288 (Iowa 1979). For example, the broker must disclose to the principal all material facts that might affect the latter's decision in a given transaction: *Flammer v. Ming*, 621 P.2d 1038 (Mont. 1980). As in the case of other agency relationships, the agency ends on the death of the agent or principal, or revocation by the principal: *Smith v. H.C. Baily Companies*, 477 So.2d 224 (Miss. 1985).

Even though the broker almost always serves as the seller's agent, not the buyer's, the broker must exercise fairness and good faith when communicating with the buyer. Intentional misrepresentation by the broker, relied on by the buyer, can be the basis of a suit for fraud and deceit, a topic explored in Chapter 4, *infra*.

The real property statutes of most states deny commissions to unlicensed brokers and courts have approved that denial (for example, *Cardillo v. Cause Extension Engineering, Inc.*, 377 N.W. 2d 412 (Mich. App. 1985)), whether or not the brokers have signed a listing agreement (*Global Resorts, Inc. v. Fanille Inc.*, 478 So. 2d 1179 (Fla. App. 1985)).

Given the type of activity brokers engage in, the license requirement is not surprising, for the public must be protected from the unscrupulous and unqualified (*Ball v. State Real Estate Division of the Department of Commerce*, 604 P.2d 113 (Nev. 1979).

All fifty states and the District of Columbia require brokers and salespersons to be licensed: their statutes detail licensure prerequisites, prohibited practices for which licenses may be revoked or suspended, and the structure and power of the administrative agencies that regulate broker and salesperson conduct—usually designated as real estate "commissions" or "boards."

With respect to license requirements all the states (and D.C.) have age, education, and experience qualifications, and distinguish between brokers and salespeople, the latter needing less in the way of credentials. The states, however, vary widely in their willingness to accept the credentials of broker/salespeople citizens of other states. In fact thirty states extend no reciprocity at all, for example, with most of the remaining states participating in reciprocity agreements with a small number of other jurisdictions.

Nine states require licensees to be bonded in amounts ranging from $1,000 (Wyoming Statutes, Sec 33-355.7(c)) to $10,000 (Montana Real Estate License Act of 1963, Sec. 66-1933). And all states charge various levels of licensure and examination fees.

As for prohibited conduct: All states proscribe false, misleading, and deceptive licensee conduct with nearly the exact same statutory language—"substantial misrepresentations," "false promises," and "pursuing a continued and flagrant course" of misconduct—grounds for license revocation or suspension. Several states specifically cite "false advertising" as a separate ground for disciplinary action; advertising is considered false when it is "misleading," "inaccurate," "untruthful," or otherwise dishonest. Of these states, several take disciplinary action only when the false advertising is done "knowingly" or "willfully." See, for example, Annotated Code of Maryland, 1957 Ed., as amended, Article 56, Sec. 224 (b).

Massachusetts and several other states require advertising brokers to identify themselves as brokers rather than principals (Mass. Board of Registration of Real Estate Brokers and Salesmen, Rules and Regulations, Article iv (1)). In some states they must also include their names in the advertising (for example, Illinois Revised Statutes 1977, Chapter iii, Sec. 5732(e) (2)).

All state statutes are vigilant about what information brokers and salespeople must disclose. Forty-seven states require that any licensee who represents more than one party to a given transaction must declare that fact to all participants. Forty-one states require a licensee who is himself a party to a transaction, directly or indirectly, to disclose to all parties his dual capacity as both agent and principal.

Alabama, California, Idaho, Kansas, Maine, Maryland, Nebraska, Nevada, Oklahoma, Texas, and Virginia insist that licensees disclose to prospective purchasers the existence of any known material defects in the property for sale.

New York, Texas, Nebraska, and Wyoming are unique among the states in requiring one particular disclosure, namely that the licensee make clear for which party he or she is acting. See, for instance, New York Department of State Rules and Regulations, Sec. 175.7; Texas Real Estate License Act, Sec. 15 (4)(D).

Eight states have incorporated into their statutes regulations specifically designated as "codes of ethics." Two—Idaho and Wyoming——have incorporated into their statutes by reference the code of ethics of the National Association of Realtors. But most states, New York and California among them, prefer to rely on their enumerated grounds for license suspension and revocation and a blanket proscription covering several general categories of undesirable behavior.

Maine's statutory language is typical: It prohibits "any other conduct, whether of the same or different character/from that of the enumerated grounds for suspension and revocation/which constitutes or demonstrates bad faith, incompetency, or untruthfulness, or dishonest, fraudulent or improper dealings." (Maine Revised Statutes, Title 32, Chapter 59, Sec. 4056 (B)).

Each state imposes some form of fiduciary responsibility on its brokers to ensure that they protect and properly account for the substantial sums of money that may pass through their hands; state regulations often prescribe detailed recordkeeping and accounting procedures that each real estate office must follow (see, for example, Colorado Real Estate Commission, Rules and Regulations, Sec. E).

Regarding broker commissions, the statutes of the vast majority of states take no position whatever on the issue. Idaho, North Dakota, and South Dakota have identical statements of policy: "The Commission...neither recommends nor recognizes any agreement to fix or impose uniform rates of commission on any real estate transaction." (See South Dakota Real Estate Commission, Rules and Regulations, Sec.20:56:02:06.).

The statutes of Ohio and South Carolina are unique in that they state that fees are to be "fair and reasonable" and determined "after discussion and negotiation with the client" (Ohio Division of Real Estate, Canon of Ethics for the Real Estate Industry, Article 15; Rules, Sec. 1301: 5-3-08).

Finally, as for sanctions imposed for violations of state law and regulations: In addition to license suspension and revocation, many state statutes impose criminal penalties for violations, ranging in severity from a $100 fine or 30 days imprisonment in Iowa (Code of Iowa, Chapter 117, Sec. 177.43) to a fine of up to $2,000 and two years imprisonment in Louisiana (Louisiana Revised Statutes, 1950, Title 37, Chapter 17, Sec. 1458).

A few states also provide for private rights of action with damage awards of up to three times the amount of commissions or profits earned as result of each violation. See, for instance Montana Real Estate License Act of 1963, Sec. 66-1940. New York allows recoveries of up to four times the illegally earned sums (New York Real Property Law, Article 12-A, Sec. 442-e(3)).

PRACTICE TIP: Review the broker/salesperson licensing law of your state, discuss it briefly with your client during the initial interview so he or she will be able to assess the conduct of the broker involved in your deal, and don't be reticent about citing it to the involved broker if you perceive a violation.

EXAMPLE: In one transaction I handled, a seller brought me a fully executed contract of sale prepared by a broker and that had the broker assuming the duty of holding the down payment until closing. By the agreement, buyer was to deliver the down payment to the broker within ten days of the contract date.

On the deadline date I contacted the broker and asked if he had received the down payment. The response was: "I expect it today or tomorrow." Two days later I phoned again and no down payment had been received. "It's coming," I was told. Ten days after the deadline the report was that still no down payment had been tendered, a material breach of the agreement.

When I demanded an explanation from the broker, he said, "Look, I'm just trying to make everybody happy." Through clenched teeth I politely reminded him that there was only one person he "had to make happy"—my client the seller. The broker then admitted that the buyer happened to be a personal friend of his (a fact he had not disclosed before), and "probably will not be going through with the deal after all."

With teeth unclenched I sternly reminded the broker that his "friend" was bound by the contract of sale and most certainly would be going through with the deal unless he wanted to suffer the legal consequences. I also referred the broker to the broker/salesperson licensing law of our state, and suggested that he review it rapidly if he wanted to stay in business.

EXAMPLE: In his official certified report to a buyer couple I was representing, an inspector wrote as follows:

> The one-car garage was in extremely poor condition. The sill plate of the garage was rotted and a section of the sill plate was missing on the rear right corner. The asphalt roof has been patched, but its total replacement will be required. The roof sheathing was rotted on the left and right sides with extensive repairs required. Several of the 2" x 4" roof rafters were rotted and in poor condition. Extensive repairs to and/or rebuilding of this garage will be required. Due to the nature and extent of the repairs, consideration should be given to replacing the garage.

The inspector put the garage repair bill at approximately $8,000. The couple relayed this information to the broker with whom they were working and to me. The broker immediately disputed the repair estimate; I immediately contacted the seller's attorney, and he and I agreed that our clients would split the cost of the repair.

But how much would that repair cost? The inspector estimated $8,000. After seeking the advice of a local contractor, the broker came in with a figure exactly half that, which the seller and his attorney adopted as their position. The seller's attorney, moreover, apparently somewhat of a handyman himself, told me that he himself had visited the garage and the local contractor was "right on target." Problem.

I then contacted my client's inspector: he stood fast in his view. I instructed my clients to do likewise and proposed to my colleague on the other side of the transaction that we escrow $2,000 from buyer tendered monies at the closing (half the disputed amount of $4,000) pending completion of the repair work for the buyers, after they moved in, by that same local contractor who had given the lower estimate. My colleague refused. "Okay," I said, "the deal is off." The seller's attorney hung up the phone.

That night, I received an anguished call from the broker telling me that I was "ruining" the deal, and that I was "way off" on the garage repair estimate. "Tell you what," I responded, "if the seller won't afford my clients the full escrow protection they seek, why don't we make a collateral agreement in which you agree to relinquish to my clients $2,000 from your sales commission should my guy's estimate prove to be the correct one." The broker hung up the phone.

The next morning, I received a call from the seller's attorney, during which he apologized for his "abrupt behavior" the day before and agreed to the escrow arrangement I had proposed. The deal closed; and when my clients met with the local contractor to plan the garage repair, he quoted them a figure of "$8,000." Why the switch? "No switch," he said, "I was told before the closing to estimate the cost of repairing only the left side of the garage." My client did not press him on "who" gave that instruction.

PRACTICE TIP: So, as usual, the wise buyer—and attorney—will beware: It's much easier to check the validity of the statements before a deal is made, than to litigate the intent and truth of those statements after closing has taken place and the deal maybe regretted.

HANDLING HUMAN RIGHTS AND FAIR HOUSING ISSUES

Not only is broker conduct bound by agency and state licensing law, and by NAR ethics: it is also bound by federal and state law seeking to create a single, unbiased housing market.

The cornerstone statute is the Fair Housing Act of 1968 (Title VIII of the Civil Rights Act of 1968, P.L. 90-284, 82 Stat. 81, 42 USC Sec. 3601, et. seq.) which makes it unlawful for brokers and virtually everybody else (single homeowners and other groups excepted under certain conditions) to discriminate on the basis of race, color, religion, sex, or national origin when selling or leasing residential property. Among the prohibited acts are:

- refusing to sell, rent, or negotiate with any given individual
- discriminating through any statement or advertisement restricting the sale or rental of residential property
- tailoring terms, conditions, or services to discriminate against any person
- stating, for a discriminatory purpose, that a dwelling is not available for sale or rental
- profiting by convincing homeowners to sell or rent because of entry into the neighborhood of individuals of a certain race, color, religion, or national origin
- denying membership or limiting the participation of people in any multiple listing service, real estate brokers' organization, or other organization connected with the sale or rental of dwellings, as a means of discrimination.

Moreover, brokers and everyone else (with no exceptions) are bound by the Civil Rights act of 1866 (Sec. 1, 14 Stat. 27, 42 USC Sec. 1982) which prohibits discrimination in housing based on *race* without exception, as the result of the Supreme Court decision in *Jones v Alfred H. Mayer Company*, 392 U.S. 409 (1968) upholding that statute; by the Civil Rights Act of 1964 (P.L. 88-352, Title II Sec. 201, 78 Stat. 243, 42 USC 2000, et. seq.) which prohibits discrimination in federally funded housing programs; and by Executive Order #11063 of November 21, 1962 issued by President Kennedy (27 Fed. Reg. 11527, 42 USC Sec. 1982) prohibiting discrimination in housing funded by FHA or VA loans.

Many states have laws that overlap the federal statutes and seek to achieve the same goals. Article 15 of New York's Human Rights Law (Executive Law), as an illustration, prohibits so-called "blockbusting"—inducing homeowners to sell by making representations regarding the entry or prospective entry of minority individuals into the neighborhood. See Sec. 296, Paragraph 3-B.

Attorney v. Broker:

The broker's relationship to both attorneys—for the seller and the buyer—is crucial to the success of any deal. Rarely is it all lollipops and roses because, although the broker's interest may parallel the interests of the other two, it will never be identical.

First, there is an often-heard broker gripe about lawyers, which, unfortunately is too often right on target. Many lawyers, brokers complain, are deal-breakers—clumsy intruders who foul up transactions because they lack a "sense of urgency." The lawyers can't be found; they don't return calls; they don't expedite their work on the contract. Because of their delays, the parties have time to change their minds and too frequently do.

Naturally, lawyers have gripes about brokers. One source of friction is over the broker's predilection for playing lawyer, especially in the preparation of documents. In general courts do not prohibit a broker from preparing listing agreements, offers, and acceptances (binders), or even sales contracts. However, with respect to contracts, most courts allow him (or her) to complete standard form contracts—that is, merely fill in the blanks—the form of which an attorney has approved. See, for example, *Keyes Co. v. Dade County Bar Ass'n*, 46 So. 2d 605 (Fla. 1950). If he goes further than "filling in the blanks," he engages in the unauthorized practice of law, and can be held in contempt of court, fined, and deprived of a commission. Even inserting a simple condition such as "seller to seed and grow a lawn" is to practice law without authority: *Martineau v. Greeser*, 182 N.E2d 48 (Ohio C.P. 1962).

As for other documents (mortgage, title opinion, and deed), the courts divide. Although some allow brokers to fill in blanks, many refuse even this. See, for example, *The Florida Bar v. Irizarry*, 268 So.2d 377 (Fla. 1972). In states where attorneys are sparse, the courts are understandably more lenient: *Conway Bogue Realty Inv. Co. v. Denver Bar Ass'n*, 312 P. 2d 998 (Colo. 1957), for example.

Whether or not the courts permit brokers to prepare agreements, whether "preparation" is defined as filling in blanks or more expansively, you can never be sanguine about papers you have not prepared or helped to prepare. You are the only true advocate your client has, the only one who can protect him fully. When he signs paper without your input—which broker-prepared papers by their very preparation encourage him to do—your advocacy has been compromised.

In New Jersey, buyers sign broker-prepared sales contracts that become legally binding at the end of a three-day period unless an attorney for the buyer or seller "revises and disapproves of the contract." (See *New Jersey State Bar Ass'n v. N.J. Ass'n of Realtor Boards*, 467 A2d 577 (N.J. 1983).) At first glance, the attorney review appears to give real estate attorneys the latitude they need to represent their clients properly. In the opinion of this writer, however, attorneys are hampered by this practice. Why do they allow only three days for the review? Are the reasons for disapproval limited? May the attorney add riders to the contract? Of course, case law addresses some of these questions. But the need for litigation shows that it is better, even in New Jersey, for attorneys to control the contract process from the very beginning.

PRACTICE TIP: How do you handle brokers? You should treat them respectfully, cautiously—and skeptically (not cynically). Try to win as much cooperation from him or her without sacrificing your client's interests. Never confuse a broker's major aim (getting to closing as quickly as possible, to earn a commission) with your number one goal (protecting your client whether or not a deal is closed). At the first contact, try to establish a friendly, collegial relationship. Thereafter, don't hesitate to be an adversary if necessary.

HOW TO DEAL WITH THE BIT PLAYERS IN A DEAL

You'll encounter other people besides the broker in the course of representing a client in a real estate transaction. They need to be mentioned here, but only briefly. *The Title Company*: Transfer of clear title to the property is a key issue to both buyer and seller, so you may have contact with a variety of title company representatives, from sales agents to title company officers to title examiners. The buyer's attorney usually has the closest dealings with the representatives, because he is the one who orders the title report and title insurance on the property for his client. Title companies rely heavily on the services of "approved attorneys" whom they retain to handle tasks such as searching title, rendering opinions on the validity of title, and performing closings.

What services do title companies perform? They do an extensive search of relevant public records to determine whether any person or party other than the seller has any right, lien, claim, or incumbrance that must be taken into account, prepare an abstract of title, and then issue a title insurance policy.

The public records they search include those containing copies of the actual deeds to the subject property, grantor-grantee index (illustrating the chain of title from all sellers to all buyers), probate records and records of intestate administration, tax records, local atlases, and even newspapers. The abstract of title they prepare is a document that refers to every deed, will, and other conveyance in the chain of title, and annotates the chain of title with reference to mortgages, liens, and other encumbrances (in chronological order).

The title insurance policy they issue—for a relatively modest, one-time premium—is a contract of indemnity guaranteeing that the title is as reported, and if it is not and the policyholder is damaged as a consequence, the company will indemnify the insured against his losses up to the face amount of the policy. The basic coverage protects against risks such as mistakes in the interpretation of wills or other legal documents, wills not probated, forged deeds, and releases.

Title company representatives frequently attend and direct the closing itself in states such as Alaska, Arizona, Colorado, New York, and Pennsylvania.

Most states require title companies to be licensed by the state; many states also require the title officers of those companies to be licensed. If you have any questions in this regard, the department of insurance of your state is most likely the place to direct your inquiry.

Inspectors: Buyers (and sometimes sellers) will frequently retain inspectors to report on the condition of property about to be purchased. Sometimes these inspectors become involved before the parties execute the sales contract, sometimes after.

General inspectors check the exterior of a structure (roof, gutters and leaders, siding, windows, steps and walkway, chimney, shrubs, property drainage, exterior foundation, driveway, entry doors, and garage) and its interior (heating system, water heater, basement, plumbing and electrical systems, appliances, and rooms). Special inspectors have a narrower function, such as checking for termites and other destructive insects.

While licenses in many states are available for such general and special inspection work, few states, apparently, require them. For obvious reasons, you should urge your clients to retain only licensed inspectors and follow these guidelines:

- Don't hire an inspector recommended by a broker unless it is inconvenient or impractical to find another. Why? The broker wants the deal accomplished: an inspector who obtains a lot of business from the broker's referrals may not be as objective as he should be; influenced by the broker, he may gloss over something that might jeopardize the deal.

- Check the inspector's credentials carefully: if he claims to be licensed, ask the nature of that license and whether it is currently in effect.

- Ask the inspector for references (apart from brokers') and a copy of one of his previous reports.

- Ask him if he is willing to sign a notarized statement at the end of his inspection report reading something like this:

> _____ assures the buyer that every reasonable effort was made to ascertain the present condition of the building through visual inspection. This inspection is the oral and written professional opinion of those conditions that existed at the time of the inspection.

If the inspection concerns termites, (and none were found), request this type of statement:

> This is to certify that _____has inspected for subterranean termites and other wood-destroying insects at the property known as _____. After careful visual inspection and sounding of all accessible exterior and interior areas, no evidence of wood-destroying insect infestation was found at the time of the inspection.

Client and inspector enter into a contractual relationship, of course, with the latter promising to perform to a certain standard and the former to pay for that performance. An inspector's report is evidence of that performance and can be used against him if in error.

EXAMPLE: A client of mine, about to purchase a relatively new condominium, hired an inspector highly recommended by her boss. When she took possession of the condo after closing, she discovered that the stove did not work at all. When she queried the inspector, he told her that, when he had inspected the premises, the seller's family "was in the kitchen eating what appeared to be hot food," so he "naturally assumed that the stove was in working condition."

Unfortunately, my client had no remedy against the inspector; for in his final inspection report he had recommended that she "inspect the stove for defects prior to closing," and she had failed to do so—despite this recommendation and my instruction, a day before the closing, to check all appliances.

    PRACTICE TIP: Sometimes an inspector can be "too good." One, for example, came highly recommended to a buyer I represented. My client was warned, however, that the inspector "loves to find things wrong—positively licks his chops when he spots a blemish of any kind to put into his report." "If you pay too much attention to his views," the warning continued, "you may never buy a home." My client retained this inspector to check three houses, and on his advice refrained from buying all three. The client finally took my advice and hired a different inspector for house number four.

Along these lines, an attorney can be "too good," squashing a deal because of technical objections that could have been overcome with business finesse. ***PRACTICE TIP:*** *Don't sweep problems under the proverbial rug: quite the contrary, hunt them down assiduously. But attempt to present them to your client not in dark isolation, but rather with suggestions as to how they might be overcome so the deal can go through.*

Bank Officials. Last on the list of bit players come bank officials such as loan officers and bank attorneys who concern themselves with mortgage-related issues of buyer and seller, and who usually are under ungodly work pressure—especially, of course, when the mortgage business is booming. You may speak to them several times by phone, and, in states such as New York, encounter one or more of them at the closing (which, in such states, typically takes place at the office of the bank's attorney or the bank itself). Depending on the transaction, you may also have dealings with a mortgage broker—an agent who earns a commission by securing mortgages for buyers.

EXAMPLE: A mortgage broker once approached me with an unusual proposition. He asked if I would like to refer buyer clients of mine to his mortgage company in return for a percentage of the fee collected by the company from my clients securing mortgages through the company. Naturally I asked the obvious: How could my clients possibly benefit from such a deal? Their total mortgage cost would have to be considerably more than what they would face if they went the conventional route by applying directly to a lending institution or through a mortgage broker who did not assess an additional attorney referral cost. He assured me that even with the attorney's cut, the clients would do better with his company.

That an attorney in such arrangement would have to disclose his financial stake to his clients, there can be no doubt. But even with disclosure, I had serious ethical objections to the proposition and rejected it.

Here is a checklist summary to close this chapter.

Deal Participants
  A. Brokers
    1. type
      (a) alternative
      (b) listing
      (c) Realtor
      (d) selling
      (e) traditional
    2. activities
      (a) straight brokerage (securing buyer)
        (i) advice
        (ii) negotiation

(b) quasi-legal (preparation of documents)

(c) recommendations (inspectors, for example)

3. legal and other controls

(a) basic agency law

(b) state licensing law

    (i) license qualification

        a. broker

        b. salesperson

    (ii) license suspension/revocation/criminal penalties for

        a. misleading advertising

        b. insufficient disclosure

        c. dishonest acts

    (iii) code of ethics

        a. integrated/not integrated

        b. integrated code—NAR, other

(c) NAR Code of Ethics

e. fair housing laws

B. Inspectors

1. type

(a) general

(b) special

2. licensed or unlicensed

3. references (broker-recommended?)

4. reports (certified, uncertified?)

C. Title Company Representatives

1. sales people

2. examiners

3. closing participants

D. Financial Representatives

1. bank loan officers

2. bank attorneys

3. mortgage brokers

4

BROKER'S AGREEMENT AND BINDER

The first stage of everyday real estate transactions very frequently begins with a formal agreement between broker and seller, and too frequently ends with an informal agreement between buyer and seller. The former is the so-called "listing" or "authorization to sell" agreement; the latter is what is known as the "binder" or "earnest money" agreement. In the majority of cases, both originate with the broker and are tendered to attorneys as *faites accomplis*.

Basically, what brokers provide is an information service: they spend money and effort acquiring, advertising, and disseminating information about property in a market composed mostly of "one-time" buyers and sellers interested in maximizing exposure of their homes, and achieving acceptable sales prices. Typically, buyers pay brokers nothing for the service; sellers pay brokers commissions pursuant to special listing contracts, developed by brokers, whenever specified conditions have been met. Typically, buyers entrust certain monies to brokers pursuant to an alleged contract, developed by brokers, to help brokers meet those specified conditions.

By law a broker, to earn a commission, must be able to establish an employment contract giving him or her the right to broker a parcel of property for that commission. *Philo Smith & Co. v. U.S. Life Corp.*, 554 F. 2d 34 (2d Cir. 1977).

In most states that contract can be oral. See, for example *Whitefield v. Haggart*, 615 S.W. 2d 350 (Ark. 1981). Responding to an increasing amount of litigation in this area, however, more and more states are moving the contract into their Statutes of Frauds and requiring it to be in writing. See Arizona Sec. 44-101; California Civil Code Sec. 1624; Indiana Sec. 33-104; New Jersey Sec. 25: 1-9; Oregon Sec. 44.580; Texas Civ. Art 6573a Sec. 28; Washington Sec. 36.010; and Wisconsin Sec. 1624.

It may be unilateral, bilateral, or executory (*Kruger v. Soreide*, 246 N.W. 2d 764 (N. Dakota 1976)), and may have a limited term or an indefinite duration (*Jasen v. Baron Industries, Inc.*, 685 S.W. 2d 330 (Tex. Civ. App. 1980)).

What information will a broker seek from your seller client to prepare a listing agreement? It will probably be data such as:

- seller's name and address
- legal description of subject property
- lot size (depth and frontage)
- room number and sizes; total square footage
- age of home
- schools, transportation, like information
- current real estate and other taxes
- amount of existing mortgage on property
- average payment for utilities
- appliances included/excluded in transaction
- preferred closing date
- zoning classification
- whether seller financing is possible
- other material information such as problems with property

On most occasions a broker will elicit listing information in the course of an interview with the seller and the only record of the information given will be in the hands of the broker. ***PRACTICE TIP:*** *Encourage your seller client to confirm in writing any data given the broker orally, so if there is any future dispute between the two, occasioned by a buyer charge of misinformation on the home, clear evidence on the issue will exist to protect your client—especially when the latter conveys information about the property's defects to the broker.*

WHAT SHOULD BE IN THE LISTING AGREEMENT

The listing agreement usually contains the following information:

1. seller details (name (s), address)
2. property description (with any unusual features)
3. asking price
4. payment provisions
   (a) down payment
   (b) mortgages to be assumed or acquired
5. conditions of broker employment
   (a) term
   (b) commission
   (c) nature of listing
   (d) broker to hold/not hold binder monies, down payment monies

As for the nature of the listing, the agreement may call for one of several options.

One is the "open listing" (sometimes referred to by courts as a "general listing")—which, as the phrase implies, permits seller to sell the property him or herself or retain additional brokers (besides the original listing broker) to accomplish the sale. The seller pays no commission if he personally sells the property without broker assistance. Otherwise, the first broker to land a buyer is the one who nets the commission. Moreover, the seller may discharge any broker at any time for any reason except to cheat the latter out of a properly earned commission.

A "net listing" (illegal in some states, such as New York) allows the broker to offer the property at any price higher than the listing price. When the broker sells the property, he pays the seller only the listed amount and retains the rest as commission.

Another variation is the so-called "exclusive agency." Here the broker works as the seller's only agent, although the seller himself may sell the parcel without liability for a commission. What if the seller secretly retains a second broker, and the latter manages a sale during the term of the first broker's exclusive agency? This is bad news for the seller: Both brokers would be entitled to a full commission.

Finally, there is the "exclusive right to sell" listing agreement, the species that provokes the most litigation in this area. From the broker's standpoint, it is the most favorable variation, for it obliges the seller to pay a full commission if the property is sold by (a) the listing broker, (b) another broker, or (c) the seller (even if the sale takes place after expiration of the term of the listing agreement—*McKay & Co. -v- Garland*, 701 S.W. 2d 392 (Ark. App. 1986)).

The broker's rights are fixed when he begins to spend time, effort, and monies to locate a buyer. Put another way, once the broker begins work, the seller no longer has the unfettered discretion to defeat the broker's commission by revoking the contract before the actual sale: *Dohner v.Bailey*, 485 N.E. 2d 727 (Oh. App. 1984).

Frequently, brokers assign their agreements to a "multiple listing service" —a pool of exclusive listings (generally exclusive right to sell) located in a central registry operated by a local association of brokers. Under this arrangement, any participating broker can sell any of the listed properties; he then shares a commission with the broker who originally contributed the listing—typically a fifty-fifty split.

Unless the listing contract specifies to the contrary, the broker earns his commission when he produces a buyer ready, willing, and able to buy on the seller's terms: *Menard v. Sacs*, 379 N.W. 2d 344 (Wis. App. 1985)

"Ready" and "willing" happen, the courts usually hold, when the broker hands the seller a valid written contract executed by the buyer, or—even less of threshold—when the buyer agrees to sign a contract or pay for the property. "Able" means financially able, not just to make the down payment seller requires, but to make complete payment of the purchase price closing the deal: *Century 21 Birdsell Realty Inc. v. Hiebel*, 379 N.W. 2d 201 (Minn. App. 1985).

To be entitled to a commission, the broker must be the procuring cause of the sale, the courts have held—for example, his efforts are instrumental in effecting the transaction between seller and buyer. And the burden is on the broker to show those efforts. As one New York court explained:

"The essential feature of a broker's employment is to bring the parties together in amicable frame of mind with an attitude toward each other and toward the transaction in hand which permits their working out the terms of their agreement. They may reach agreement without his aid or interference…A broker 'negotiates' just as much when he brings parties together in such a frame of mind that they can by themselves evolve a plan of procedure, as when he himself carries on the discussion and personally induces an agreement to accept a specific provision." *Baird v. Krancer*, 246 N.Y.S. 85, 88; quoted in *Salzano v. Pellillo*, 165 N.Y.S. 2d 550, 553, 1957.

A federal district court agreed that a certain broker was the procuring cause when he was the first to alert a buyer that the subject house was for sale, had set up meetings between buyer and seller, had accompanied the buyer on a tour of the house, and had zealously pursued the deal until the buyer actually made the purchase. *Reines & Co. v. Erimanga Investments, N.V.*, 622 F. Supp. 13 (D.D.C. 1985).

As Professor Rohan points out in his treatise, *Real Property Practice and Procedure* (Matthew Bender & Co. 1981), the connection between a broker's efforts and the accomplished transaction is a question of fact: "as long as it can be shown that the broker was the predominant moving force that led to the sale, he is entitled to a commission" (at page 14-8). Hence: If broker A finds a buyer candidate, negotiates a substantial agreement, and then broker B works out the details and closes the deal, broker A would be considered the procuring cause and the one entitled to the commission.

A broker may collect a commission where he had agreed to bring the parties together and leave the negotiations to them, and fulfilled that obligation.

A broker may collect a commission even if the seller voluntarily reduces his sales price for a prospective buyer brought to him by the broker.

A broker may collect the commission if he is the moving force in the sale, even if the seller refuses to sign the contract of sale, and even if the seller signs and later breaches the contract by refusing to perform under the deal. See *Century 21 Birdsell Realty Inc. v. Hiebel, supra.*

Consider this hypothetical: A broker shows a condo to a buyer candidate. The buyer rejects the condo but alerts a friend to its availability; and this friend buys the property. Is the broker entitled to a commission. The answer is "most likely," on procuring cause grounds.

Note, however, that if the broker works out a general agreement between a prospective buyer and seller, but has a disagreement with the seller and abandons the project, a second broker if he completes the agreement would be entitled to the fee, not the original broker.

PRACTICE TIP: *Avoid the ready/willing/able and procuring cause traps with a simple strategem. When drafting a listing agreement, include a phrase such as "The broker's commission shall be deemed earned and shall be payable at the completion of closing (if any), and the proceeds of the sale shall be the sole source of the commission payment."*

This language protects the seller who refuses to execute a sales contract with a qualified buyer, or a seller who executes and then breaches the contract. Unfortunately, as already mentioned, what happens all too often is that a seller executes a listing agreement before consulting with counsel and makes himself vulnerable to the traps just described.

PRACTICE TIP: *Remember that the amount of the broker's commission is always negotiable.* Although six percent or seven percent of the purchase price are the most common commissions (according to a recent survey done for the Federal Trade Commission and my experience), these percentages are not set in concrete: advise your clients to seek a lower rate; often, just by raising the issue, they will accomplish a 5.5 or 5 percent rate. When the listing agreement does not expressly mention the rate due, the courts will allow a broker a "reasonable" fee as determined by the standards of the given community: *Robertson v. Humphries*, 708 P.2d 1058 (Okla. 1985).

The Binder

Few legal rules are as simple, direct, and mandatory as the rule about binders, documents brokers have a propensity to prepare.

PRACTICE TIP: *WARN YOUR CLIENTS NOT TO SIGN THEM—PERIOD!*

This is a book about practical real estate law; and so I would be justified ending the discussion right here. I can't and won't for a practical reason: Clients often sign binders before they retain you, and they become your problem.

Why are binders so dangerous? First, let's look at a little background. A binder is a species of writing or memorandum attempting to outline what broker, seller, and buyer—although not necessarily the courts—consider the basic real estate bargain, the so-called "offer and accceptance." Brokers prepare it because they think it will secure a commission—sellers sign it because they think it will secure a sale—buyers go along and sign too because they think it will preserve the purchase.

The trouble is that binders do all of the above, some of the above, and none of the above depending on whether they qualify as binding contracts, and on other factors. Unfortunately, as to whether they are binding, you only know for sure after a lawsuit. Courts generally hold that they are binding contracts of sale if there was a meeting of minds on all of the elements of a proposed sale (parties, subject matter, mutual promises, consideration) and none were left for future negotiation: *Phillips v. Johnson*, 514 P.2d 1337 (Ore. 1973).

But, enforceable or not, binders rarely contain all the protections for both sides that a properly drafted, formal contract can provide. Even patently unenforceable binders can work against your clients—sellers in particular—for such binders may be construed as indicating an intent to pay a brokerage commission, making them liable to pay a commission even though, because of the unenforceability, the property is never sold.

Whether any given binder will be deemed enforceable is simply not easy to predict. As we have said, they must contain all of the elements of the proposed sale; however, this needs further explanation.

First, the binder must describe the property with reasonable certainty, or at least offer a shorthand description that can be supplemented with admissible parol evidence (section, block, and lot number designations may do the trick).

Next, it must set forth the terms of buyer's payment clearly and unequivocally. State courts construe the payment clarity issue differently. Georgia, for instance, would find too indefinite language such as "the price is $130,000, subject to a mortgage of $60,000." Connecticut would have no quarrel with such language.

In most states if the binder calls for a purchase money mortgage (that is, one the seller grants the buyer) but neglects to state the interest rate, it will be unenforceable. New York and New Jersey follow the minority rule in this regard: they will imply interest at a reasonable rate with payment of the mortgage due on demand. No state, furthermore, will enforce a binder calling for payment of the purchase price "at a future time," with no date specified.

What if the closing date is omitted? Most courts would simply fix a reasonable date. What if the buyer and the seller agree to close "at a mutually agreeable time"? Here the binder would fail, for an essential contractual element is missing. What happens if no place of closing is stated? Most courts would instruct the parties to close at the office of the seller's attorney or at the seller's residence. Other omitted terms such as utility and tax apportionments and lesser matters most courts would supply, whether the parties liked it or not.

What about exculpatory language such as "subject to a formal contract" or "details to be worked out?"

The latter phrase would probably not prevent the binder from serving as a binding contract; the former is problematic. If the document reads "the parties shall not be bound until the execution of a formal agreement," there is no contract no matter how solid the rest of the binder. See, for example, *Ripps v. Mueller*, 517 P. 2d 512 (Ariz. App. 1973). If it reads "this writing shall not be effective until and unless it is specifically approved by the buyer's attorney," again, there is no contract. All the parties have in these two cases is an "agreement to agree."

EXAMPLE: One day, an elderly priest phoned an attorney friend of mine with a problem. When his sister died a few months ago, he said, he inherited from her a small house which he promptly listed with a broker. He intended to donate the sale proceeds to the poor of South America through the Maryknoll Missionary Community.

Within two weeks of listing, the broker found a buyer, and had the priest and the buyer execute a binder in contemplation of a formal sales agreement, or so the priest thought. Thereafter, before the priest's attorney could circulate a sales contract, a member of the priest's parish offered the old gentleman $50,000 more for the property. On the advice of his then attorney, he executed a formal contract of sale with the second buyer and notified the first that he would not be accepting his "offer" after all.

The attorney for the first buyer immediately slapped a *lis pendens* on the house and brought suit for breach of the binder "contract." Explaining that he went into the second deal only because he thought that it would raise that much more money for the poor, the priest asked my friend if he should fire his lawyer. My friend said "no" and advised prayer.

NONEXCLUSIVE LISTING AGREEMENT PROTECTING THE SELLER

1. The "seller" (or "sellers") is/are_____.

2. The "broker" is _____, who is duly licensed as a broker under the laws of the state of _____.

3.The "property" is a one/two/three/four family house located at _____. The sale of the property includes the following items of personal property_____

_____.

4. This agreement operates as a listing of the property with the broker, and employs the broker as real estate broker for the property. The property is to be sold at a price of at least $_____, payable as $_____ down and the balance at closing. The seller(s) is (are) willing/unwilling to provide financing to the buyers. The seller(s) has (have) the right to change the asking price of the property at any time, without liability to the broker.

5. The listing under this agreement is not exclusive. The seller(s) retain(s) the right to list the property with other brokers, the broker with a multiple-listing service. The Seller retains the right to sell the property him/her/themselves without a broker.

6. This listing continues until the broker has sold the property, or until the seller(s) notify(ies) the broker that the listing is cancelled. The seller has the right to cancel the listing and/or remove the property from the market at any time before a contract of sale is signed.

7. The broker will be entitled to a commission of_____percent of the purchase price, payable at the closing, if and when all of these events happen:

• The broker was directly or indirectly responsible for procuring the buyer and for the negotiation and consummation of the contract of sale

• The seller(s) and qualified buyer(s) have entered into a contract of sale, on terms and conditions acceptable to the seller(s). The seller(s)'s judgment as to whether terms and conditions are acceptable is final and binding.

• The transaction actually closes, the full purchase price is paid, and title is conveyed to the buyer by bargain and sale/warranty/quitclaim deed subject to the terms, covenants, and conditions of the contract of sale.

8. Despite the provisions of Section 7, above, the broker will not be entitled to a commission if the transaction fails to close because:

• The owner does not have good title and cannot convey good title as required by the contract of sale.

• for any reason other than the seller(s)'s willful default. If the transaction fails to close because of the buyer's willful default, the seller will have no obligation to pursue legal remedies to enforce the buyer's obligations under the contract of sale.

9. This agreement constitutes the entire agreement between the seller(s) and broker. This agreement can be modified only by a written agreement signed by both seller(s) and broker.

Date:_____, 19____ Signatures: Seller(s): _____

Broker: _____

5

THE CONTRACT OF SALE (PART I)

The formal contract of sale sets forth the terms and conditions of the real estate transaction, fixing promises and performances, and dates for both. It is a dynamic, rather than static, document to which both sides must refer again and again as the transaction unfolds up to and through closing—the blueprint and power source of the deal.

The Statute of Frauds in most states requires the sales contract to be in writing, a writing which can be in the form of letters or telegrams, note or memorandum, or several writings to be construed together. Of course, the writing can be drafted from scratch in more formal fashion.

The writing most attorneys use, however, is a two-part document consisting of printed boilerplate provisions and one or more rider attachments altering the boilerplate. Title companies, financial institutions, brokers, and legal stationers issue such documents drafted to standards set by local custom and state law (for example, "plain English" requirements imposed by some states). Most attorneys prefer them, for convenience (rider additions are far less work than a whole new draft) and general reliability (much of the language has been tested in litigation).

PRACTICE TIP: Often forms are tilted in favor of buyer or seller; so be sure to read every word of every form carefully and look to correct any tilt adverse to your client.

We will divide our discussion of the sales contract into two sections. Part I, this chapter, will cover most of the major provisions of the typical house sales agreement (type of writing notwithstanding); Part II, the next chapter, will review the remaining provisions of this contract and conclude with a few words about the condo and co-op agreements.

ESSENTIAL TERMS

Date: The sales contract begins with the date of the contract—that is, the date the parties decide the contract "was made" (regardless when either or both executed the document). It is significant because it is the marker for those time-related obligations assumed by the parties, especially the buyer.

To illustrate: If the deal is contingent on an attorney's review, or on an engineer's or termite inspection, the seller traditionally allows the buyer "x" number of days "from the date hereof," the contract date, to accomplish that review or inspection. Note that few deals are all cash transactions; most contracts are contingent on buyer mortgage financing, and this usually becomes the most vital contingency of all. Sales contracts typically give buyer a certain number of days from the contract date to obtain a loan commitment, failing which the deal is terminated. (Much more about this later.)

Names: The seller's name(s) and address usually come first, the buyer's immediately thereafter. There are two questions regarding the seller's identification to keep in mind. One, is the named party vested in a marketable title he or she can convey, or is there an unnamed party lurking in the shadows who could legally block conveyance of the title? Two, does the named seller have the capacity to make the conveyance?

The first question, as framed, suggests half of its solution. You must quiz the seller carefully to determine who is likely to assert an adverse interest; and if you uncover such a person, you then have to help the seller negotiate with that person—an ex-spouse, for example, who may have a right by way of a tenancy by the entirety or dower.

Capacity becomes an issue most often when the seller is an infant. In most states an infant's conveyance is voidable, that is, valid until voided by the infant grantor when he or she reaches majority. It is voidable even if infant conveyed the property to an innocent purchaser for value (maybe your client). Capacity is also a red flag when the seller is:

- a charitable organization (court approval may be required)
- a partnership (conveyance may have to be made in partnership name)
- a corporation (stockholder approval may be necessary)

Suppose an agent wants to sign the contract on behalf of the seller?

States such as New York require an agent's authority to execute on behalf of the seller to be in writing; others, such as Rhode Island, permit the authority to be by parole. ***PRACTICE TIP:*** *The safe approach is to insist on a written power of attorney from the agent, executed and acknowledged in proper form for recording.*

With respect to the buyer's name (s), capacity to contract and agency can be issues as well: the seller must know who he or she can hold liable for the purchase (and purchase money mortgage, if any) and when.

When a married couple buys a home in a great many states, they usually take title as tenants by the entirety—on the death of either, title to the entire property passes immediately to the survivor by operation of law, regardless of any will. States without tenancy by the entirety accomplish the same end through a survivorship deed.

PRACTICE TIP: *Here is a word of caution: Courts in more than half the states interpret any conveyance to two or more parties as creating a tenancy in common unless there is specific language calling for a tenancy by entirety or joint tenancy.* Thus, if your clients are buyers taking a parcel of property as husband and wife, be sure that the names on the sales contract and deed read, "Brian Russell and Lisa Russell /for instance/ husband and wife."

EXAMPLE: A client couple of mine sought to purchase a house clearly beyond their means; so they persuaded the husband's brother to act as co-obligor on a mortgage loan they wished to apply for at a local bank. The bank approved the loan on the condition that the brother's name be included in the contract and deed as a third purchaser, which meant that the brother would actually be taking title to the house with the couple.

I objected to the condition, arguing that it was in no one's best interest, including the bank. A minor squabble between the brother and the couple could cause the former, as a tenant in common, to move to partition the property. Then the property would be sold out from under the couple. When the bank refused to waive the condition, the couple followed my advice and applied for a mortgage at another bank that did not have such a condition; and they were successful.

Description of the Property: In a transaction the size of a real estate sale, the seller naturally must know precisely what he is selling, the buyer precisely what he is buying. ***PRACTICE TIP:*** *Inasmuch as the seller's attorney usually prepares the first draft of the sales agreement, he or she has the obligation to describe the property accurately in the first instance.* Where does the description come from? It can be taken from the seller's deed, an old title insurance policy, an opinion of title, a certificate of registration, and any other papers associated with the property.

You will encounter two common types of descriptions: block and lot numbers on a filed map, and metes and bounds. *PRACTICE TIP: If you represent a buyer and receive a block and lot number description, consult the related filed map or an existing survey to check the numbers; if you receive metes and bounds, plot out the description, starting at the "place of beginning" and proceeding clockwise around the boundaries of the tract and referring to linear measurements and directions until you are back to the place of beginning. By doing this exercise, you can uncover any errors that exist and have them corrected before closing.*

PRACTICE TIP: Be especially careful of vague and approximate descriptions of rural property, which may refer to natural elements such as creeks, brooks, hills, and pastures that change over time. Consider as an illustration *Sessions v. Cowart*, 601 SW2d 82 (Tex. Cov. App. 1980). In this case the Court denied specific performance of a sales contract because the description, "Brick Home owned by Effie Cowart—Location 2½ miles on the left of the Airport Road (Lost Scott Road) West of US 96," was too vague in the Court's opinion. If your client is buying rural property, have a careful, new plot plan prepared and attach it to the sales contract as an exhibit.

Often descriptions end with a paragraph that reads something like, "being the same premises conveyed to the seller by the deed dated and recorded in the office of the Register of the City of _____, County of _____, in Reel _____, page ____ and by street number ____."

What this language does is to indicate the seller's chain of title; and according to some state court decisions will cure an otherwise faulty description of property being sold. Even if does not provide a cure, it will help determine the parties' intent if one side sues for reformation of the contract.

Printed forms, moreover, often include provisions such as:

"This sale includes all of the Seller's ownership and rights, if any, in any land lying in the bed of any street or highway, open or proposed, in front or adjoining the premises to the center line thereof. It also includes any right of Seller to any unpaid award by reason of any taking by condemnation or for any damage to the premises by reason of change of grade of any street or highway."

Why the language appears has a two-part explanation. The usual property description does not carry the fee to the center line of the street (assuming the property fronts on a street); and the buyer, not the seller, deserves any monies subsequently awarded for condemnation or damage in connection with the street bed.

Personal Property: The standard sales contract obligates seller to sell not just the real property described as we mentioned above, but also all his or her personal property appurtenant to that real property. In this context "real property" simply means land and buildings. "Personal property" includes items such as plumbing, heating, lighting, and cooking fixtures, bathroom and kitchen cabinets, shrubbery, fencing, ranges, refrigerators, and air conditioning equipment.

PRACTICE TIP: While a deed may be sufficient to convey personal property, it does not pass title to it. Hence you want language in the contract such as, "The sale also includes all fixtures and articles or personal property attached to or used in connection with the premises," followed by a detailed list of those fixtures and articles.

Whether any given item is actually "appurtenant" to the subject property is a question of fact: the detailed list eliminates any ambiguity on this score. ***PRACTICE TIP:*** *This list is fully negotiable, of course, with the seller the party, typically, with the greater negotiating leverage.* For instance he may want to take the washer/dryer with him when he moves: therefore, he can simply omit it from the sale, knowing that the contract price does not include such items unless they are specifically identified in the contract, and that such an omission is unlikely to prejudice the overall deal in any event.

Sometimes a seller can effectively use personal property as bargaining chips. Let's say he instructs his attorney to omit from the contract personal property list any reference to air-conditioning units and a dishwasher. And let's say the buyer signs the contract subject to an acceptable engineer's inspection, and the inspection turns up a defect in the property that buyer wants reflected in a lower contract purchase price. The seller may then agree to include in the sale all of his air-conditioning units and the dishwasher in consideration for the discovered defect, and thereby preserve the original purchase price.

Requiring the seller to provide a bill of sale for personal property is not the usual practice—but your buyer client may need one in jurisdictions that tax the sale of personal property not acquired for resale. These jurisdictions require the buyer to pay the tax and the seller to collect it.

PRACTICE TIP: *End the personal property provision of the contract with a precise list of personal property excluded from the sale (usually furniture and household furnishings); and include a statement to the effect that no part of the contract price is allocable to personal property included in the sale—unless allocation is required for tax purposes or the personal property represents a relatively substantial proportion of the value of the sale. Include the additional statement that the buyer can purchase none of the personal property unless title to the real property is closed.*

Purchase Price: Most form sales agreements set out the purchase price, and the stages and conditions of its payment, in a neat delineation that minimizes the potential for misunderstanding (and litigation).

They divide the price into (a) a down payment payable, typically, on execution of the contract (by check subject to collection); (b) an allowance for unpaid principal on an existing mortgage or deed of trust; (c) the amount of any purchase money note and mortgage from seller to buyer and (d) a balance due at closing.

What is there to say about reciting the purchase price beyond the obvious? Check it with your client and make sure it is typed correctly on the contract. Be aware, furthermore, that it may need renegotiation if the contract has been made subject to an inspection and that inspection uncovers a defect the parties had not previously considered and may want to apportion money for; or if before closing the property is destroyed in whole or in part by fire or other disaster.

With regard to the down payment, most jurisdictions define it as a payment "on account of the purchase price." This means that, should the buyer default on the contract, and the contract does not otherwise speak to remedies for breach, the buyer forfeits the entire down payment—even if the seller cannot show actual damages stemming from the buyer's breach.

How much money does buyer traditionally put down, and why should the amount concern you?

As a rule the down payment is a percentage of the purchase price—often 10 percent, sometimes less, seldom more, and always negotiable. *PRACTICE TIP: From the buyer's standpoint, the greater the down payment, the more investable capital he ties up until closing (often months down the road), and the more he may lose if the deal founders. From the seller's standpoint, the down payment size is a measure of the buyer's willingness to close the transaction (rather than walk away from it and forfeit his deposit), and his financial strength (and ability to qualify for a mortgage).*

While, as we have said, the buyer traditionally plunks down the down payment on execution of the contract, he can certainly negotiate another arrangement. A buyer client of mine, as an illustration, persuaded a seller to accept her deposit monies in two stages—five percent on execution, and five percent one month later when she closed her condominium sale, and had more cash with which to work.

Who holds the down payment until closing is a critical issue for buyer. If it is the seller (by the sales contract), and he defaults, many jurisdictions without qualification grant the buyer an equitable lien on the subject property in the down payment amount. The buyer may foreclose the lien as an equitable mortgage—if the seller holds an estate in the property. Otherwise, buyer has no lien, only an action against the seller personally for the down payment monies.

Suppose the seller executes the contract, collects and banks buyer's deposit, and thereafter conveys the contract property to another innocent purchaser for value? Who obtains the property, buyer 1 or buyer 2; and what happens to buyer 1's down payment?

PRACTICE TIP: In many states, including perhaps your own, where recording of the sales contract is permitted, a seller may successfully convey to a second buyer (if, for example, the second offers a higher price after the contract with the first buyer is signed), unless the first buyer's attorney had the foresight to record his client's contract of sale with the seller. If said attorney did not, the first buyer has no equitable lien on the property, only a direct action against the seller in personam against seller for the down payment. In these states, recording establishes constructive notice to others of an original buyer's rights and gives the buyer the protection of a vendee's lien against the land should seller attempt to convey to a new buyer.

That the seller is not the ideal party to hold buyer's down payment should be clear from the above. Who, then, should hold it? In a good number of states the broker does the honors. In my judgment, he or she is not an ideal choice either—and for fairly obvious reasons. For one, the broker is the seller's agent and can be expected to tilt in favor of the seller in a seller/buyer dispute, perhaps even to the point of obeying an unjustified (and maybe illegal) seller instruction to withold the return of the down payment when buyer demands it. Remember, too, that the broker's aim is to collect a commission, which usually does not happen unless there is a closing: he may use his custody of the down payment as leverage against a party intent on ending the contract before closing—forcing a buyer with marginal financial strength, for example, to accept a mortgage deal more onerous than a deal the buyer originally contemplated making (but for which the buyer proved to be unqualified).

Unless the contract of sale or other agreement clearly binds the broker to a careful and proper administration of the buyer's down payment—and few do—a broker should not be entrusted with these monies.

A far better candidate is the seller's attorney, and, in many states, he or she almost always assumes this task—usually pursuant to carefully drafted escrow language in the sales contract, contract rider, or separate escrow agreement. The language traditionally defines the attorney as a stakeholder, nothing more, nothing less, liable only for negligence in handling the money and damages if he defies a court order directing its disposition. It specifies when the money must be released and to whom under normal circumstances: to seller when seller delivers the deed at closing, or to buyer when buyer is entitled to a preclosing refund (for example, if buyer is unable to obtain a mortgage).

PRACTICE TIP: If the parties vote for an interest-earning escrow, reasonably concluding that someone other than the bank should receive the interest, naturally try to secure all of the interest for your client. If you are unsuccessful, accept a split of the interest payable at closing. And if you are the stakeholder, remember that taxes will be due on that interest unless you set up a special account in the names of both buyer and seller.

Many form contracts specify that the stakeholder must place the downpayment monies in a noninterest bearing account until closing to avoid a dispute over who is entitled to the interest on the monies at closing—buyer or seller—and simplify the stakeholder's bookkeeping life (no year-end taxes on escrow interest).

Mortgages: A buyer may satisfy the purchase price in part by assuming the seller's existing mortgage or taking a purchase money mortgage from the seller. *PRACTICE TIPS: If you represent the buyer you want to make sure that an existing mortgage is described completely in the sales contract—mortgage sum left unpaid, date of maturity, interest rate, and so forth. In fact, it is probably wise to attach a copy of the mortgage to the contract as an exhibit.*

By definition, a purchase money mortgage is one the seller writes (not a bank or other lending institution) as a concession to a buyer who cannot otherwise finance the purchase. In duration it can be short-term gap financing until buyer acquires permanent financing, or long-term financing like a conventional mortgage. Because it serves as an incentive for buyer to buy, it is not a loan *per se*, in the view of most courts, and hence not subject to usury laws (in most states).

PRACTICE TIP: The seller's attorney traditionally draws the "PMM", and if that's you, be sure to require the buyer to make monthly deposits covering real estate taxes, and grant your client, the seller, the right to accelerate the maturity of the principal if the buyer defaults.

If you are on buyer's side of the transaction, review the PMM draft before your client signs the sales contract, when his bargaining power is greatest. Negotiate for the right of buyer to prepay without penalty; and insist that the entire set of papers be attached to the contract as an exhibit. If your client also needs a conventional mortgage to make the deal work, determine whether the lending institution being approached will allow the subordinate lien of a purchase money mortgage on the property.

Balance Due at Closing: When there is a shortfall in the purchase price payoff, that is, after the down payment and existing mortgage and PMM monies are totalled, it is satisfied by an additional sum set forth in the contract. The buyer agrees to pay this sum in cash, his own good certified check, or any official bank check. For obvious reasons, the seller's attorney usually insists that any cash to be delivered will be limited in amount, and that any checks tendered will be drawn on a local bank or trust company. In the usual deal, existing mortgages and PMMs are not involved; and the lion's share of the "balance due at closing" will come from conventional mortgage funds referred to in the contract rider (more about this later).

Title Company Approval: Most contracts obligate the seller to give and the buyer to accept such title as a reputable title company is willing to approve and insure under its standard form of title policy—and rightly so.

Title companies approve and insure what is called "marketable title," that is, title free from defects and encumbrances in the chain of title. "Defects" may stem from a deed in the title chain that was improperly executed, or executed by an incompetent grantor, or delivered after an improper will probate, or that was rendered defective in some other fashion. "Encumbrances" include matters such as unpaid taxes (real estate, transfer, estate, or franchise), liens (for example, mechanic's liens), water charges, judgments, executions, attachments, restrictions on property use, encroachments, and unpaid leases.

Practically speaking, the technical distinction between defects and encumbrances is not especially significant. For a title company may be unwilling to approve and insure title if it spots any type of burden in the chain of title interfering with the transfer or use of the subject property or subjecting it to any kind of obligation.

Substantial Law on Title Defects: When is a title unmarketable? In one case a combination of four mortgages, two financing statements, and an oil, gas, and mineral lease certainly added up to defects of title rendering the title unmarketable, where they were not mentioned in the sales contract or earmarked for satisfaction out of sales proceeds, (*Bailey v. First Mortgage Corp. of Boca Raton*, 478 So.2d 502 (Fla. App. 1985). In this case the buyers received their deposit back after they elected to terminate the sales contract for failure to deliver marketable title. Actually under the contract the sellers had a period to cure these defects; but they waived it by telling buyers they had received a higher competing offer and would terminate buyers' contract if buyers did not match that competing offer.

Similarly, the buyer in *Grace v. Nappa*, 389 NE2d 107 (N.Y. 1979) agreed to take the property subject to an existing mortgage, under a sales contract obligating the seller to produce an estoppel certificate at the closing evidencing the balance of the mortgage, interest rate, and other relevant facts about the loan.

At the closing, the seller did produce a letter from the bank holding the mortgage, but it stated that the loan was not in good standing. Not surprisingly, the buyer refused to close and sued for the return of the down payment—and prevailed. The court held that the seller's failure to convey the property with the existing mortgage in good standing was a failure to convey good title and a breach of the sales agreement.

Determining the sufficiency of title is the buyer's responsibility, and yours if he (or she) is your client. ***PRACTICE TIP:*** *If you represent the buyer, order a title search from a reputable title company (and there are plenty around), or at least understand completely why a search is unnecessary.* Without such a report and subsequent title insurance, your client will be limited to whatever warranties appear in the deed and other deeds in the chain of title.

In the unusual case of *Page v. Frazier*, 449 N.E. 2d 148 (Mass. 1983), the plaintiff signed a mortgage application stating that the lender's attorney represented the lender's interests, and that the buyer, if he wished, could retain his own attorney. The buyer neglected to do this.

The bank's attorney searched and approved the title, which turned out to be unmarketable. The buyer sued the bank's lawyer for detrimental reliance, and lost—it was clear that the lawyer involved represented the bank only, and the buyer had no right to rely on him.

Title Company Examinations: Title companies investigate the ownership history of property as it passes from one owner to the next in the chain of title. That history is often contained in numbered volumes, stored in the registry of deeds, containing copies of all recorded documents. The title company checks the grantor-grantee index to those volumes, finds the relevant documents, and studies them looking for a potential cloud on title. The company may also check probate and tax records, and other records (for example, the motor vehicle department's records of traffic tickets) for any recorded defect or encumbrance.

Abstract of Title: Depending on local practice, buyers' attorneys order either an "abstract of title" or a "certificate of title" from the title company. The abstract is a complete, condensed history of the title, including a summary of all recorded instruments and all problem areas. The certificate, also called a "letter of opinion," is issued when the title company is willing to state that title is good and marketable.

Here is a condensed version of a typical certificate of title: "XYZ Title and Guaranty Company certifies to Milktoast Esq./ Buyer's Attorney/ that, in consideration of the fees due and payable upon the delivery of this certificate, it has examined the title to the premises described in Schedule A herein, in accordance with its usual procedure and agrees to issue its standard form of fee policy in the amount of x dollars/the price buyer is paying for the property insuring such interest and the marketability thereof, after the closing of the transaction excepting all loss or damage by reason of the estates, interest, defects, objections, liens, encumbrances, and other matters set forth in this certificate which are not disposed of to its satisfaction prior to the closing of title or issuance of the policy."

This provision dovetails with another requiring the buyer's attorney to notify the seller's counsel of any cloud on title, that the title report shows, within a fixed period of time, so that the seller can attempt to remove the cloud—failing which the parties' contractual remedies come into play.

Title Defects: Some clouds on title are routinely removed at the closing. This can be done either by instruments properly executed by the seller, in recordable form, necessary to lift the cloud, delivered to the buyer at closing (with appropriate recording or filing fees); or by the seller's direction to the buyer to pay and satisfy the encumbrance out of the cash the buyer delivers at closing. This seller's direction is also the usual way that liens arising out of unpaid taxes, water charges, and the like are extinguished.

Title companies approve and insure title "subject to" some matters set out in a separate contract clause. It usually provides that the sale is "subject to covenants and restrictions of record provided that the same are not violated by existing improvements and use thereof does not render the title unmarketable." Although these covenants and restrictions may technically be defects or encumbrances, they are generally acceptable to the buyer. Here are some examples.

- laws and governmental regulations affecting the maintenance of the property
- consents for erection of structures on , under, or above streets abutting the property
- encroachments of stoops, areas, cellar steps, trim, and cornices on any street or highway
- utility companies' rights to maintain and operate lines, wires, cables, poles, and distribution boxes in, over, and upon the property.

PRACTICE TIP: If you represent the seller, try to incorporate language in the contract excepting "any state of facts a personal inspection of the property would show" and "any state of facts an accurate survey would show."

If you represent the buyer and the "accurate survey" reference appears in the "subject to" provision, you may want to order a new or updated survey of the property in addition to the title examination. Then there'll be no surprises as to the dimensions and location of the land your client is buying. In any event, if your client is financing the purchase through a bank or other lending institution, the institution will often require a new or updated survey in addition to the title examination.

Form of Deed: A separate provision in the contract of sale obligates the seller to transfer full ownership of the home in question to the buyer, in return for the buyer's tender of the full purchase price. The actual transfer occurs when the seller delivers to the buyer a deed in proper statutory form, ready for recording.

Note: No convenants of any kind are implied in a deed. Therefore, the buyer's attorney will negotiate for a deed with covenants protecting his client. His first choice is a full covenant and warranty deed that specifies that the seller is seized of the property in fee simple and has good right to convey it; the buyer will quietly enjoy the property; the property is free from encumbrances; the seller will procure any further necessary assurance of title; and seller will forever warrant title. In this buyer-oriented version, the buyer will have the right to sue the seller for damages for any violations of these covenants and warranties, whether or not they are directly caused by the seller.

In the real world, and for obvious reasons, the seller's attorney will oppose giving a full covenant and warranty deed. The seller wants to end the transaction at the closing, with no continuing liabilities to the buyer or any future grantee of the buyer who may cause trouble many years later.

The seller's attorney prefers a bargain and sale deed—one that confirms the bargain struck (property in exchange for consideration) and the sale made (transfer after payment), and is sufficient to pass title to the property. The seller's attorney will usually prevail, because he can make the valid argument that the buyer is adequately protected in any case by his examination of title and by title insurance.

PRACTICE TIP: If you represent the buyer and accept contract language specifying a bargain and sale deed, you might want to add, "with convenants against grantor's acts." This language gives the buyer the assurance that the seller did nothing during the course of his possession of the property that would render title unmarketable (and that might be missed by a title examination). But, except in rare cases, you should settle for nothing less than a bargain and sale deed.

In the rare case that the contract of sale is silent on the required form of deed, the buyer would be required to accept a quitclaim deed at closing. This form of deed purports to convey only the seller's present interest in the property (if any)— not the property itself. In effect, it does not obligate the seller to the buyer in any way; it doesn't even imply that the seller has title at all, much less good title. If the seller does have title, it can be passed by quitclaim deed; if not, no title will be conveyed.

Closing Date and Place: Almost every contract of sale contains a clause such as: "CLOSING will take place at the office of _____ at   , o'clock on _____ 19____." You just fill in the blanks on the contract and mark the date down in your appointment book.

Usually the date is introduced as an "on or about" date, not set as a certain date. The precise time of closing is dictated by the busy schedule of the lenders who are involved in most transactions. The closing will have to be delayed if the mortgage commitment hasn't been issued to the buyer yet; or even if the lender's attorneys are not available on the scheduled closing date.

As for the place, local custom rules. Closing in many states takes place at the office of the lender's attorney; at the office of the seller's attorney, if there's no mortgage.

If the contract is silent as to time of performance, the law implies that the closing will take place within a reasonable time of the face date of the contract. In this context, reasonableness depends on the particular circumstances of the contract.

Suppose, however, that the time fixed for performance is vital to one of the parties—let's say because the property's value is fluctuating rapidly, or the buyer needs the property right away, or the seller needs the proceeds to discharge a maturing obligation or close on another property. In other words, how is the question of the closing date handled when "time is of the essence?"

The general equitable principle is that time is not of the essence unless the contract expressly states that it is (*Freeman v. Boyce*, 661 P. 2d 702 (Hawaii 1983). ***PRACTICE TIP:*** *It's rarely prudent for the parties to state this.* Delays are very common in real estate transactions. Both sides know it, and can make adequate provision for delays. There are also "players" involved whose actions the parties cannot control: the lender, for instance.

However, if time is indeed of the essence and the contract so states, and if the seller is not ready, willing, and able to perform on the scheduled closing date, the buyer is excused from performance under the agreement and is entitled to the return of the entire down payment. If the seller is ready, willing, and able to perform, but the buyer is not, the buyer stands to lose all rights under the contract, including the right to return of the down payment.

Risk of Loss: Earthquake, flood, fire, hurricane, or other casualty causing accidental loss of the property between the date the contract is fully executed and the closing: if the contract is silent on the issue, who's stuck with the wreckage or the ashes? Is the buyer or the seller on the spot?

A minority of the states answer that the seller is stuck: the theory is that the subject matter of the contract has to exist when time for performance arrives at the closing. If the subject matter is destroyed, the contract terminates, and the buyer is entitled to return of this down payment. The seller must rely on insurance proceeds—or on personal and family financial resources if there is no insurance.

Surprisingly, most states force the buyer to go through with the deal if the contract is silent as to the risk of loss. The buyer bears the loss and can only be made whole if he is wise enough to protect himself with insurance as soon as the contract of sale is signed. The theory in these states is that, when the contract is signed, the buyer becomes the owner of the "equitable" title of the property; the seller holds only bare legal title in trust for the buyer pending closing. As equitable owner, the buyer must suffer the risk of loss.

Provisions in many form contracts aim to avoid the problem by fixing the risk on one side or another—usually the seller's. Because of the swirl of litigation in this area, the Commissioners on Uniform State Laws have formulated the Uniform Vendor and Purchaser Risk Act (U.V.P.R.A.). Under this Act, when a contract does not speak to risk of loss, the risk is on the seller pending transfer of either possession or title to the buyer. The Act also distinguishes between material and immaterial loss and stipulates the rights of the parties in each case.

A number of states have adopted the U.V.P.R.A. New York, for example, has enacted it as General Obligations Law Sec. 5-1311, which reads in full as follows:

> 1. Any contract for the purchase and sale or exchange of realty shall be interpreted, unless the contract expressly provides otherwise, as including an agreement that the parties shall have the following rights and duties:

> a. When neither the legal title nor the possession of the subject matter of the contract has been transferred to the purchaser: (1) if all or a material part thereof is destroyed without fault of the purchaser or is taken by eminent domain, the vendor cannot enforce the contract, and the purchaser is entitled to recover any portion of the price that he has paid; but nothing herein contained shall be deemed to deprived the vendor of any right to recover damages against the purchaser for any breach of contract by the purchaser prior to the destruction or taking; (2) if an immaterial part thereof is destroyed without fault of the purchaser or is taken by eminent domain, neither the vendor nor the purchaser is thereby deprived of the right to enforce the contract; but there shall be, to the extent of the destruction or taking, an abatement of the purchase price.

> b. When either the legal title or the possession of the subject matter of the contract has been transferred to the purchaser, if all or any part thereof is destroyed without fault of the vendor or is taken by eminent domain, the purchaser is not thereby relieved from a duty to pay the price, nor is he thereby entitled to recover any portion thereof that he has paid; but nothing herein contained shall be deemed to deprive the purchaser of any right to recover damages against the vendor for any breach of contract by the vendor prior to the destruction or taking.

> 2. This section shall be so interpreted and construed as to effectuate its general purpose to make uniform the law of those states which enact it.

> 3. This section may be cited as the uniform vendor and purchaser risk act.

Form agreements in U.V.P.R.A. states are likely to include a provision reading something like: "This contract form does not deal with the question of what happens in the event of fire or casualty loss before the title closing. Unless another provision of this contract provides otherwise, the Uniform Vendor Risk Act will apply. One part of that law makes a buyer responsible for fire and casualty loss upon taking title or possession of the premises."

Warning: The Act is no panacea. For one thing, it gives no guidance on which losses are "material" and which are "immaterial" (so your drafting should clarify this point). For another, it appears that the seller cannot enforce the contract against the buyer if there is a material loss—but the buyer can enforce it against the seller without an abatement of the purchase price.

A neat solution—if you represent the seller—is to remove the risk of loss or taking by condemnation or eminent domain outright. How? By focusing on the disposition of the award or insurance proceeds if a loss or taking occurs by including a clause that supersedes the U.V.P.R.A. Draft the provision to say that, if there is a preclosing casualty, and the seller has not made a complete repair or restoration by closing, the buyer is entitled to the net proceeds of the insurance or award (less the seller's cost of repair or restoration). Any uncollected proceeds are allocated to the buyer.

The case of *Long v. Keller*, 104 Cal.App.3d 312, 163 Cal.Rptr. 532 (1980) highlights these issues. The plaintiff leased the property in question with an option to buy. Over the six-year course of the lease, the plaintiff made extensive improvements in contemplation of purchase of the property. When the plaintiff exercised the option, he put the earnest money in escrow with a note, secured by a deed of trust, for the balance of the price. The sales contract obligated the plaintiff to buy a fire insurance policy payable to the defendant-seller. The plaintiff failed to do so, and the property was destroyed by fire before the closing.

The defendant returned the down payment, and tried to rescind the contract. The plaintiff sued for damages in the amount of the proceeds of the fire insurance policy prudently maintained by the defendant. The defendant was granted rescission under the U.V.P.R.A., because a plaintiff in possession has all the risk of losses not caused by the seller; the seller had a continuing equity interest entitling him to the insurance proceeds.

6

THE CONTRACT OF SALE (PART II)

The first part of our discussion of the contract of sale (Chapter 5) covered in some detail many of the major elements of such contracts—names of the parties, property description, personal property in the deal, purchase price components (down payment, mortgage, cash), title company approval, form of deed, date and place of closing, and risk of loss.

In this chapter, we focus on the remaining elements found in the sales contract—the so-called "conditions," the closing adjustment provision, and certain key miscellaneous provisions almost always present in it. The chapter also offers brief examinations of typical condo and co-op contracts, and a relatively simple, representative sample, contract of sale form showcasing the elements discussed in this and the previous chapter.

But almost half of the chapter is devoted to what the parties view as the unthinkable, their attorneys conceive as improbable, and the courts know as all too common—litigation stemming from disputes over the contract.

CONDITIONS OF SALE

Sales contracts are frequently conditioned on certain kinds of performance. Performance of each condition is a condition precedent to other obligations under the agreement; and if the performance does not occur, the buyer is usually entitled to a return of his (or her) down payment. Words such as "if" and "subject to" tip off the presence of a condition, and these words and the full condition statement may appear in the printed form, boilerplate section of the contract. More likely, however, they will be found in riders prepared by the seller's attorney in the first instance, and modified by buyer's counsel in the second.

A sale may be contingent on a buyer receiving satisfactory results of tests and inspections (for example, electrical, engineering, septic system, gas leak, soil, well-water). It may be contingent on the sale or closing of the buyer's present home, or on the buyer obtaining a license to use the premises. The buyer's attorney may have to approve a sales contract prepared by a broker, executed by the buyer. Finally, the sale may be conditioned on the seller's delivery of certain documents at closing, such as a certificate of occupancy (a document issued by a local government indicating that a building complies with public health and building codes).

Termite Inspection: This provision is virtually standard in contracts in the Northeast (and in other areas of the country where termites are prevalent). In essence, it allows the buyer to cancel the agreement if he does not receive a satisfactory termite inspection report. (The buyer orders, and pays for, the report.)

PRACTICE TIP: Sellers' attorney will want to modify the provision so that their clients will have the option either to repair any termite damage found by the report, or cancel the agreement; and can allow the buyer to purchase the damaged house without repairs, but with an abatement of the purchase price.

Without the provision, buyer can generally rescind the contract if the house is damaged by termites, because the intended subject of the contract is an un-damaged house. The buyer has been granted rescission either on a theory of innocent misrepresentation of material fact by the seller (for example, *Halpert v. Rosenthal*, 267 A.2d 730 (R.I. 1970)) or mutual-mistake (for example, *Davey v. Brownson*, 478 P.2d 258 (Wash. App. 1970)).

As an illustration of the complexity of problems that can arise in this area, consider *Mercer v. Woodard*, 166 Ga.App. 119, 303 S.E.2d 475 (1983). There were five defendants: four associates of a realty company, and a fifth person who had joined them in buying and rehabilitating a house for resale. The would-be buyer sought an FHA (Farmers Home Administration) mortgage on the property. The FHA demanded certification from the sellers that there was no termite damage. The sellers offered a letter stating that no live termites were found. This did not satisfy the FHA; finally one seller produced two acceptable letters.

However, it turned out that the house was extensively damaged by termites. The plaintiff-buyer successfully sued the sellers, the realty company, the renovator, and the exterminator for fraud and conspiracy to defraud, and was awarded $22,000 in actual, $150,000 in punitive damages. The award was affirmed in full on appeal, with the appellate court holding that defendants sued on a conspiracy theory can be subjected to punitive damages even if not all of them are found guilty of the conduct constituting the conspiracy.

Mortgage Contingency

Certainly the most critical condition in the sales contract is the one that makes the contract conditional on the buyer's obtaining a written commitment for a conventional mortgage from a lending institution by a stated date. The time frame within which a bank may be expected to review and rule on an application, and which will be acceptable to a seller, may range from as little as two to as much as six weeks (or even more). If the buyer fails to receive the commitment in time, the contract is automatically cancelled and his or her down payment is returned.

The typical mortgage contingency provision gives the buyer 30 to 45 days to achieve a commitment, with extensions of the deadline at the seller's option.

Buyer's Obligation

The buyer is usually obligated to:

- make prompt applications and do those things necessary to obtain a commitment
- accept the commitment when issued
- notify the seller of the proposed lender's name and address
- send the seller a copy of the commitment when it is issued.

The seller may also be granted the right to seek alternate financing for the buyer if the buyer is unsuccessful on his own.

The courts have held that the mortgage contingency provision obligates the buyer to make a reasonable effort to seek the commitment, otherwise the down payment will not be refundable after a failed application.

As you might expect, there is considerable case law defining "reasonable effort." In general, a buyer need not accept a mortgage commitment calling for unreasonable installment payments, or to accept two separate mortgages or a mortgage for a smaller amount than he intended to finance. Nor will the buyer be penalized for providing truthful information that dooms a mortgage application, or for withdrawing from the deal because a change of circumstances reduces the income previously believed available to carry the mortgage.

The buyer is obligated to act responsibly—for instance, he or she can't back out of a deal, claiming inability to obtain "adequate financing" where loans on the stated terms are available in a nearby city. The buyer can't insist on finding financing in his own home town (*Moore v. Moore*, 603 S.W.2d 736 (Tenn.App. 1980)).

Where the contract obligated the buyers to seek assumption of the mortgage and, if the seller's bank denied this, to enter into another arrangement, the buyers' failure to apply for approval of the assumption caused them to lose their rights to specific performance of the contract or return of their down payment. The sellers in this case offered title free of defect; the buyers were in breach by not seeking assumption, and therefore the down payment constituted liquidated damages: *McDaniel v. Kudlik*, 598 S.W.2d 350 (Tex.Civ.App. 1980).

However, unless the contract mandates it, the buyer is not obligated to accept a purchase-money mortgage from the seller after being turned down by several banks: *Senese v. Litz*, 471 NYS2d 401 (A.D. 1984). Furthermore, to be acting in good faith, a buyer need not make a (useless) formal application after being informed that funds are not available to him—and the buyer need not settle for an available "swing loan" in lieu of permanent financing to comply with the mortgage contingency clause: *Nolley v. Harris* 176 Ga.App. 553,336 S.E.2d 822 (1985).

But the buyer is in breach of the mortgage contingency clause if he refuses to apply for a mortgage located by the broker (*Ng v. Simons*, 495 NY2d 456 (1985)). The clause, as it is usually drafted, does not say that the buyer has to find the financing himself-only that he must make a good-faith effort to achieve it.

In another case involving a broker, *Burnett v. Brito*, 478 So.2d 845 (Fla.App. 1985) (this time an interpleader action brought by the broker holding the down payment), the buyer was not in default by not applying for a mortgage within the 60 days specified by the contract. Relying on the broker's representations, the buyer applied for an assumption of the seller's mortgage; once the 60 days were up, he tried hard to obtain a regular mortgage commitment.

However, the buyer was not entitled to damages in the amount of the cost of mortgage applications, lost wages, and travel expenses, because the contract did not contemplate such damages. Nor could the buyer use a clause awarding him specific performance and attorney's fees on default by the seller to recover his attorney's fees—for the failure to close was caused by the buyer's inability to achieve financing, not by the seller's default.

Hanson v. Moeller, 376 N.W.2d 220 (Minn.App. 1985) involved another facet of the interaction between the broker and the mortgage contingency clause. The holding in this case is that the clause is for the benefit of both the buyer and the seller, and its enforcement must be waived by both of them for the clause to be inoperative. Where the seller makes it clear that he will not waive enforcement and the buyer has not obtained a mortgage, the deal is off; there is no enforceable contract. Therefore, the broker has not produced a buyer ready and willing and able to buy—and has not earned his fee.

But where the seller agrees to extend the time for obtaining the mortgage commitment, and the buyer gets the commitment within the time as extended, the seller has no right to rescind the contract, and the buyer is entitled to specific performance: *Livote v. Mallon*, 81 AD2d 533, 438 NYS2d 81 (1981).

Importance of Timing

This brings us to the issue of timing—an issue that has led to extensive litigation. Compare *Kalik v. Bernardo*, 439 A.2d 1016 (Conn. 1981) with *Loda v. H.K. Sargent and Associates*, 188 Conn. 69, 448 A.2d 812 (1982), for instance.

In *Kaklik*, the contract called for a financing commitment "to be obtained no later than April 23, 1975 [an arbitrarily chosen date with no intrinsic significance] or this agreement shall become null and void and deposit money returned to buyer." The would-be buyer (and eventual plaintiff) managed to acquire the commitment on April 23, and sent a notification letter to the defendant seller on April 24. The seller, who wanted to back out anyway, used the delay in notification as a pretext to cancel the contract.

The court granted plaintiff specific performance, holding that the slight delay was no justification for backing out of the contract; the defendant's excuse, that inflation made specific performance untenable (housing prices had risen significantly in the meantime) was invalid, because, said the court, post-contract events and circumstances are irrelevant.

However, the sellers prevailed in *Loda*. In that case, the buyers agreed to buy a house for $74,000, with ten percent down. The contract was made contingent on the buyer's achieving a conventional mortgage of at least 25 years' duration, for $59,000, at not more than 11 percent interest, on or before March 12, 1979. The sellers were obligated to oust the tenants then living in the house on or before May 1, 1979.

The buyers managed to acquire a commitment on March 14, but only for $55,000. They notified the sellers of this commitment, told the sellers to eject the tenants, and applied for an increase in the commitment. However, the bank turned them down, and buyers proceeded to back out of the deal.

The result was that they forfeited their down payment. The court held that the buyers waived the financing condition when they demanded removal of the tenants; loss of the down payment was a fair penalty for the sellers' loss of opportunity to find another buyer.

In *Schultz v. Topakvan*, 473 AD2d 91 (1984), the mortgage contingency clause called for a commitment on or before August 28, 1984. The buyers received a commitment on August 25, when they were vacationing, and failed to notify the sellers until September. (Their letter, dated September 1, was received on September 3.) In the meantime, the sellers, who had not been notified of the commitment, informed the buyers that the deal was off. The buyers were denied specific performance at the trial level, but won on appeal.

The court decided that the contingency clause (which was intended, at least in part, to protect the buyer) applied to obtaining the commitment, not telling the sellers about it. Anyway, a letter notification to seller within three days was held to be reasonable notice, particulary in light of the fact that the sellers were told orally before August 25 that the commitment was pending.

PRACTICE TIP: *Keep close contact with your clients so you can assess progress toward* *the financing commitment. Be especially vigilant during the summer and around the Christmas holiday season—don't let notices go unsent because the bank officer or your client (or you yourself) is on vacation.*

Damages and Other Remedies

The real estate lawyers objective is to make the deal succeed—to ensure that a fair contract is drafted and executed, that the parties perform their respective obligations, and a timely closing occurs, when the buyer pays the price and the seller transfers the title.

However, not all deals succeed. One of the parties may refuse, for whatever reason, to perform his obligations for example; and unless the contract speaks to the circumstances, the aggrieved party must appeal to the law and its remedies to enforce those obligations.

Let's examine the remedies before we go on to consider a useful contract language.

Specific Performance

When there is a breach, specific performance is available to both parties on certain conditions. This is the favored remedy when money damages would be inadequate or when the property in question can't be replaced by another of equal value. ***PRACTICE TIP:*** *This remedy is discretionary with the court; and it's not available if the sales contract is grossly unfair, the remedy would cause unacceptable hardship or loss to the party forced to perform, or if the plaintiff has unclean hands.*

For instance, a developer of a condo project can't accomplish specific performance if the buyer decides he doesn't want his unit after all—in this case, monetary damages are perfectly satisfactory: *Centex Homes Corp. v. Boag*, 320 A.2d 194 (N.J. Super. 1971). The developer in that case was permitted to enforce a contract provision calling for forfeiture of the down payment.

But compare that to the co-op developer in a factually similar case, *Silverman v. Alcoa Plaza Associates*, 323 NYS2d 39 (A.D. 1971). The developer did not win specific performance either, and in addition was required to show actual damages before retaining the down payment after a default by the buyer.

The case of *Godwin v. Lindbert*, 300 N.W.2d 514 (Mich. App. 1981) shows how hard it is for the attorney to anticipate everything that could go wrong with a deal. The buyers (the Godwins) agreed to buy the Lindberts' house. The contract included a mortgage contingency clause based on an 8 ¾ percent mortgage. The Godwins received the commitment, and appeared on the scheduled closing date. However, Mr. Lindbert didn't appear—the sellers were in the throes of a divorce, and Mrs. Lindbert had gotten an injunction forbidding her husband to close with the buyers.

Angry Mrs. Lindbert refused to convey the property; and, as time passed, mortgage rates rose and rose until the best rate the Godwins could get was 11 ½ percent. The angry Godwins sued for specific performance and won. They were also awarded damages equal to the difference in the mortgage rates, on the ground that the damages were a predictable consequence of the delay in closing.

Rescission

A seller who failed to disclose a material fact—for example, that a lakefront lot is below a state-owned flood easement, and thus unfit for residential use—was estopped from demanding specific performance of the contract. The buyers could not discover this fact by ordinary care and diligence; once they did, they naturally wanted out of the deal. They were awarded rescission of the contract, plus interest on the down payment dating from the time of the payment: *Smith v. National Resort Communities, Inc.*, 585 S.W.2d 655 (1979).

The remedy of rescission is easily defined. It is the undoing of a contract without penalty to either party, placing each bank in his precontract position. It is the proper remedy, say the courts, where there is a mutual lack of knowledge about a property's tendency to flood, for instance, and mutual misunderstanding about the property's suitability for the buyer's needs: *Carter v. Matthews*, 701 S.W.2d 374 (Ark. 1986).

However, even with a mutual mistake, rescission was unavailable where a lessee and potential buyer undertook substantial improvements to the property—it was no longer possible to return the property to its original condition: *Derouin v. Granite State Realty, Inc.*, 459 A.2d 231 (N.H. 1983).

In appropriate cases, rescission can combine with other remedies. As an illustration, in *Reed v. King*, 193 Cal.Rptr. 130 (Ca. App. 1983), plaintiff-buyer sued for rescission and damages when she discovered that her new house had been the scene of a multiple murder ten years earlier. She brought an action against the seller and the real estate agent (who not only knew about the history but asked a neighbor to keep mum about it). The defendants won at the trial level, but the plaintiff prevailed on appeal. To the appellate court, the plaintiff had made out a fraud case; the defendants had a duty to disclose the information, which was material enough to affect the value of the property, and deprive the plaintiff of quiet enjoyment.

On a less dramatic note, the plaintiff in *Rodriguez v. Leonard*, 477 So.2d 19 (Fla.App. 1985) was awarded rescission, plus a vendee's lien for the money advanced, with prejudgment interest, on a contract of sale for a house to be built. The seller expressly warranted that the project violated no applicable building codes; the house would conform to the plans submitted; and the vendor would give marketable title—none of which was true.

Damages

Alternatively, either party may elect to sue for damages. The general measure of damages is "loss of the bargain" sustained by the nonbreaching party. This is usually calculated as the difference between the contract price and market value of the property at the time the deed was to be delivered. See, for example, *Guitreau v. Juneau*, 479 SO2d 431 (La.App. 1985).

A lot depends on which side breaches the contract. Assume the seller is the culprit. Unquestionably, the buyer is entitled to recover the down payment, with interest. This issue is well covered in Milton R. Friedman's *Contracts and Conveyances of Real Property* Third Edition (Practicing Law Institute, 1975). In addition, many states allow recovery of the loss of bargain plus reasonable expenses (for example, title search, termite inspection, engineer's inspection, even attorney's fees). Some states (such as New York) restrict damages to loss of bargain only (including interest on the down payment), on the theory that this measure of recovery is the equivalent of the realty buyer sought to buy; the expenses for the purchase are deemed to be the buyer's responsibility: *Schultz & Son, Inc. v. Nelson*, 256 N.Y. 473, 177 N.E. 9 (1931).

In cases of breach by the seller, a number of states (including New York and Pennsylvania) follow the so-called "good faith rule." If the seller cannot convey the property because of a defect in title, but otherwise acted in good faith, the buyer is limited to recovering the deposit plus reasonable expenses. But if the seller acted in bad faith (for example, knew about a title defect when the contract was executed, but failed to inform the buyer), the buyer is entitled to the down payment, interest, the loss of the bargain, and reasonable expenses (unless the state follows the New York rule described above). In states without the "good faith rule," the buyer is entitled to a full complement of damages (loss of bargain, down payment, interest, expenses) whenever the seller breaches because of a title defect—whatever the seller's conduct or motive. The Friedman treatise, cited above, explores this issue in more detail in Section 12.2(a)(2).

Now let us assume that the buyer breaches. Most states permit seller to keep the down payment (plus any accumulated interest)—and, of course, the property itself. Beyond this, the seller can seek his loss of bargain (if the value of the house declined in the interim) and expenses, such as attorney's fees, connected with the failed deal. However, these damages are credited against the retained down payment. (See, for example, Friedman Section 12.1 (c)). By the way, it is immaterial that the seller may have sold the property to someone else after the buyer's breach, even at a higher price. It's also immaterial that the buyer rejected title in good faith but erroneously.

For instance, in *Webster v. DiTrapano*, 494 NYS2d 550 (1985), the buyer refused to close, lacking the money to pay for the home. This breach was not excused by the buyer's inability to sell his New Jersey house—the contract of sale was not contingent on that sale—even though the contract did have a financing commitment clause, and the financing commitment depended on the sale of the house. The court determined the measure of damages to be the difference between the contract price and the market price at the time of the breach—not the sale price of the home eleven months after the breach. The plaintiffs took reasonable steps to mitigate damages by putting the property back on the market when the time of the mortgage commitment expired. The plaintiffs were under no obligation to lease the property to the would-be buyers until the buyers' affairs could be untangled.

(Interesting related issues are raised by *Crummer v. Berkman*, 499 A.2d 1065 (Pa.Super. 1985), holding that there's a jury question as to whether the buyer can avoid the contract of sale for fraud where the seller, with no guarantee of success, promised to sell the buyer's house at a price equal to the contract price—and where the buyer relied on this representation and failed to make the contract contingent on the sale of the buyer's house at the contract price or higher.)

The purpose of the remedies of specific performance and actual damages is to place the nonbreaching party, as nearly as possible in the position he would have been in had the breaching party performed the contract fully.

However, specific performance is hard to obtain from courts, and damages, as mentioned above, can be difficult to ascertain. To cope with these difficulties— and as a way to avoid ligation completely—parties often add a liquidated damages clause to the contract.

The buyer protects himself with language limiting the seller's remedy on default to retention of the down payment as sole damages.

PRACTICE TIP: *If you represent the seller, never let the buyer stipulate for less than the down payment!*

The seller protects himself by incorporating language reading that the buyer's sole remedy on default is the return of the down payment plus interest and reasonable expenses.

Possession

Remember: The essence of a real estate transaction is the transfer of title and possession from seller to buyer for the contract price. The title transfer, by definition, occurs at the closing ("closing of title"). Transfer of possession, however, can occur before, at, or after the closing.

Where the contract of sale is silent on the issue, many state courts have held that closing is the earliest time at which the buyer can take possession. However, Alabama courts are a notable exception to this rule: see, for example, *Lobman v. Sawyer*, 37 Ala. App. 582, 74 So.2d 502, state cert. den. 261 Ala. 699, 74 So.2d 205 (1954). Most contracts do cover the issue, and stipulate to possession at closing or within a specified number of days thereafter. Even if the contract contains such a clause, buyers routinely allow the sellers a reasonable time to vacate after the closing if departure on the scheduled date is impossible.

Contracts that permit possession by the buyer before closing can generate major headaches for the seller. If the buyer proceeds to default on the deal and refuses to close title, the seller usually must use the lengthy and expensive process of ejectment to evict him. Eviction via summary proceedings is unavailable to him because the relationship is one of vendor-vendee, not landlord-tenant. If the seller is the one to default (even in good faith—for instance, discovery of a title defect that seller cannot cure), the buyer can remain in possession with no liability for rent—again, because the buyer is a vendee, not a tenant.

Now suppose the seller remains in possession after the date mutually agreed on orally (subject to contract language calling for possession on closing) or in writing (by contract language calling for a transfer of possession a certain number of days post-closing). What happens then?

In some states (such as New York), the buyer has the automatic right to evict the seller by summary proceedings, even though there is no landlord-tenant relationship. See, for example, New York Real Property Actions & Procedures Law 713(8). Other states require the cumbersome remedy of ejectment unless buyer can prove that a landlord-tenant relationship that was intended for the holdover period had expired.

PRACTICE TIP: If you represent the buyer, and the seller seeks to transfer possession after the closing, you can skirt the problem by insisting that the contract stipulate a daily, steadily escalating, sum the seller must pay during any hold-over period. After a time, the sum will grow to be so prohibitive that the seller simply won't be able to afford to stay in occupancy.

Closing Adjustments

Most contracts of sale contain a provision such as: "The following are to be apportioned as of midnight of the day before the CLOSING:

1. rents as and when collected,
2. interest on existing mortgages,
3. premiums on existing, transferable insurance policies and renewal of such policies expiring prior to closing,
4. taxes, water charges, and sewer rents, on the basis of the fiscal period for which assessed,
5. fuel if any, and
6. vault charges, if any."

The contract may also call for a water meter reading on a certain date, so that a fair apportionment of water charges can be made.

This provision appears because the seller collects all profits and pays all costs on the home while he owns it (that is, until the day of the closing). The buyer collects and pays from the closing date thereafter. However, rent payments and the obligation to pay bills seldom coincide with the closing date, so apportionment between the parties must take place.

PRACTICE TIP: If the contract is silent in this regard, apportionment will not be required—so be sure to add such a clause if the form agreement does not include it.

Insurance premiums are seldom much of a problem. Usually, the seller cancels his policy and the buyer acquires one of his own. As for taxes, most of the information you'll need will come from the buyer's title report. As I've said previously, outstanding taxes constitute clouds on title, and must be removed before the title company will issue a policy.

Miscellaneous Provisions

A common provision in form agreements states that the premises are sold "in their present condition, subject to reasonable use, wear, tear, and natural deterioration" between the contract date and closing. ***PRACTICE TIP:*** *Buyers' attorneys often insist on qualifying the language by adding "at the time of the delivery of the deed the roof will be in good condition and the heating and electrical systems will be in good working order." Sellers' attorneys tend to accept the additional language with the word "good" deleted from it—a fair compromise.*

How much must the seller disclose about the condition of the property?

The vendor has an obligation to disclose facts materially affecting the value of the property, which are not known to the purchaser and are not readily observable: *Johnson v. Davis*, 480 So.2d 625 (Fla. 1985). The buyers in *Russow v. Bobola*, 2 111. App.3d 837, 277 N.E.2d 769 (1972) never asked if the basement flooded, but they asked, and were told, that the drain outside the basement was adequate. In the resulting lawsuit, the court denied defendants summary judgement because the sellers knew about the tendency to flood, and washed and painted the basement to conceal it, creating an issue of fact as to the existence of fraud.

The contract may also contain a "merger" clause, indicating that all prior understandings and agreements between the parties are merged into the contract at hand. The purpose of this clause is to assure the parties the protection of the parole evidence rule, and make it clear that all changes to the agreement must be made in writing.

Why bother to require that amendments be in writing, when the Statute of Frauds generally offers enough protection against claims of oral modification allegedly agreed to by the parties? The problem is that, under certain circumstances, the aggrieved party may be estopped from relying on the statute as a defense. That's why you should press for the inclusion of such a provision.

Drafting to Avoid Problems

If the history of litigation teaches us anything, it is that nothing can be taken for granted. The parties in *Lovelace v. Stern*, 297 N.W.2d 160 (Neb. 1980), signed a preprinted form contract calling for a purchase-money mortgage, leaving a blank space in the mortgage clause detailing the interest to be charged on the outstanding balance of the loan. The vendor sued, demanding reasonable interest. He lost: The court held that the parties intended that no interest would be payable. Because the clause was neither ambiguous nor vague, parole evidence of intention was not admissible.

If seller financing is involved, make crystal clear what form it is to take. In *Strout Realty, Inc. v. Benson*, 699 S.W. 2d 795 (Mo.App. 1985), both parties intended a purchase money mortgage and the contract called for conveyance free of liens and encumbrances. The seller insisted on consummating the transaction with a "wrap-around deed of trust," and the buyer balked. (In several states, the mortgage instrument is known as a deed of trust; the most common form of wrap-around instrument is one that carries with it the obligation to make payments on a preexisting instrument, plus additional amounts. Wrap-arounds are often used where assumption is unavailable, and the purchase price is significantly higher than the mortgage balance.)

The buyer, the court held, was entitled to the return of his down payment, even though she refused to tender the balance of the purchase price at closing. The problem could probably have been avoided by closer communication between the lawyers for the respective sides; if the buyer's lawyer knew that a wrap-around deed of trust was being prepared, rather than the conventional purchase money document, perhaps he could have resolved the problem during the preclosing period.

A complex fact pattern was involved in *Glass v. Anderson*, 596 S.W.2d 507 (Tex 1980). The parties entered into a real estate contract. Two weeks later, the buyer said he couldn't achieve financing, and had his attorney issue a written notice of repudiation. The seller demanded performance.

Eventually, the buyer did secure financing; when he notified the seller, the latter refused to close. Litigation ensued, and the court held for the seller. The seller chose not to treat the repudiation as an anticipatory breach; thus, the buyer could retract the repudiation. However, for the deal to go through, the buyer had have to retracted within the time specified for performance in the contract. The buyer didn't accomplish the financing until after the time limit of the mortgage contingency clause had expired. The seller had no duty to perform, and thus the buyer could not prevail.

PRACTICE TIP: Before your client signs a contract, "walk through" the contract, focusing not only on its explicit provisions but on its implicit meaning as well. Think of every possible "glitch" you can imagine—defects in the property; a change of heart on the buyer's or seller's part; unavailability of financing, or delays in securing a mortgage commitment; increase or decrease in the house's market value or prevailing interest rates; tax law changes; defects in title either unknown or concealed by the seller; buyer's difficulties in selling his existing home; seller's difficulties in acquiring a replacement home. Make sure the contract safeguards your client's position.

THE CONDO CONTRACT

The concept of the condominium has already been discussed, in chapter two; so it would be helpful to review that discussion before considering the special nature of the contract of sale for a condominium unit, the basic boilerplate form of which we briefly consider here. As you'll recall, a condominium unit involves fee simple ownership of an individual unit in a multi-unit-project—unlike a house, which stands on its own.

So, the first unique element in a condo contract is the description of the property at issue. The contract will state that it is a residential condominium unit known by a certain name in a building known by a certain name, together with a stipulated percentage interest in the common elements of the condo project described in a certain declaration recorded on a given date in a given county at a particular liber and page. The contract will also detail the number of rooms the condo unit contains.

Like the typical contract for sale of a house, the condo contract will detail the items of personal property included in the sale. However, the latter will go on to say that the condo sale includes whatever ownership interest the seller may have in plumbing, heating, electrical, and other central systems, and in property held by the board of managers in the name of the condo project.

The title exceptions in a condo contract (that is, encroachments on title that do not constitute grounds for rejecting title) include the condo declaration, all matters referred to in the declaration, by-laws, the condominium's other rules and regulations, and any power of attorney given to the board of managers.

Furthermore, the seller of a condominium unit makes certain representations to the buyer at the time of closing that the seller of a house does not make. The condo seller usually represents that:

- the condominium has been validly created.
- no right of first refusal by the board of manager is outstanding.
- if there are any alterations or additions to the unit being sold, all required approvals from the board and governmental units have been received.
- no assessments or major increases in common charges are established or pending against the unit due to improvements, acquisitions, or claims against the board of managers as a consequence of those improvements, assessments, or claims.

The concept and mechanics of apportionment are identical to those in conventional house deals; however, common charges on the condo unit and unit owners' association dues are additional items that must be apportioned when a condo transaction is involved.

At the closing, the condo owner is generally obliged to deliver the following documents:

- deed in a form complying with the relevant state law (for example, there may be a requirement that the deed set out a covenant to comply with the state's lien law).
- bills of sale, guarantees, and other documents sufficient to transfer to the buyer all the ownership interests specified in the contract of sale.
- (optional) certificate of insurance under any master policy insuring the condominium project as a whole.

- (optional) forms for any powers of attorney or other documents required by the board of managers.

THE CO-OP CONTRACT

In chapter two we discussed the most popular co-op concept: the one in which the tenants of a multiple dwelling own shares in a corporation holding title to the real property of the co-op complex. This section discusses the basic sales contract form for the purchase and sale of that type of co-op.

Ownership of co-op stock carries with it a proprietary lease and obligations much like those incurred by tenants of rental apartments. Thus, the first element distinguishing a co-op contract of sale from the contracts for sale of a house or a condominium unit is the description of what is being sold. A standard description clause in a co-op agreement reads something like this:

> Seller agrees to sell and transfer and Buyer agrees to buy (i) x number of shares in the XYZ Apartment Corporation allocated to Apartment 3Q in the cooperative building, located at (address); and (ii) the Seller's interest, as tenant, in the proprietary lease for the Apartment, which lease is appurtenant to the shares.

What warranties can a buyer expect a seller to grant under such a contract? That:

- seller is the sole owner of the co-op shares and the proprietary lease.
- shares and lease will be free and clear of liens at the closing.
- seller has the unfettered right to transfer shares and lease to the buyer.
- shares were duly issued to and fully paid for by seller.
- lease will be in full force and effect at closing.

The co-op seller represents to the buyer that amount of monthly maintenance ("rent") seller is paying, and covenants that, at closing, there will be no violations of record that the tenant would be obligated to cure under the terms of the proprietary lease.

In the contract of sale, the buyer represents that he has examined (or waived the right to examine) the certificate of incorporation, co-op bylaws, and the form of the lease, and is satisfied with them. He will further represent that he has read (or waived the right to read) the co-op corporation's last audited financial statement.

All co-op contracts of this kind contain language dealing with the corporation's right to approve or reject the contemplated sale. Most obligate the buyer to provide the co-op's managing agent with names and addresses of character references and parties who can attest to the buyer's financial well-being, and to appear for one or more personal interviews. They also detail what happens if the corporation approves or refuses a would-be-buyer.

If the answer is "yea," the contract will obligate the seller to assign and transfer the shares and lease to the buyer, and the buyer to pay the purchase price and to assume all of the terms, covenants, and conditions of the lease and be bound by the corporation's by-laws, rules, and regulations. To that end, the buyer must give the corporation an agreement at closing containing such assumptions. The corporation may also require the buyer to execute a new proprietary lease.

If the corporation says "nay," the contract of sale generally provides that the contract is automatically cancelled, and the entire down payment returned to the buyer.

The contract also lists the documents that the seller is obligated to deliver to buyer at closing, such as:

- seller's certificate for the shares, duly endorsed for transfer or accompanied by a separate duly executed stock power, with necessary stock transfer stamps attached. The corporation may also require a guarantee of the seller's signature.

- seller's duplicate original of the proprietary lease, with a duly executed assignment of the lease to the buyer.

- evidence that the co-op corporation has approved the transfer of the lease and shares to the buyer—usually, a certificate from the secretary of the corporation.

- a managing agent's statement that maintenance fees and special assessments due and payable to the corporation have been paid to the date of the closing.

- keys to the outer door of the apartment.

The contract of sale for a co-op often directs the seller to pay the managing agent a processing fee (for services in connection with the sale) and the legal fees of the corporation's attorney. The buyer is usually responsible for any sales and transfer taxes and for securing any title insurance the corporation or lending bank may require.

"Rent" and utility charges under the proprietary lease are apportioned as of midnight on the day preceding the closing; assessments are generally not apportioned but are payable by the party who owns the apartment when those assessments become due and payable.

SHORT CONTRACT OF SALE (RESIDENTIAL HOUSE)

1. (Date) The date of this contract is _____), 19_____.
2. (Parties) The "seller(s) is/are _____ [Husband and Wife], of _____. He/she/they own the property to be conveyed as sole owner/tenants in common/joint tenants/tenants by entirety. The "buyer(s)" is/are [Husband and Wife], of _____
_____.

The buyer (s) will take title as sole owner/tenants in common/joint tenants/tenants by the entirety. All parties are of full age and capacity to contract.

3. (Property to Be Conveyed) This contract of sale concerns a plot of land, _____ feet by _____ feet, located at street address _____, block and lot number _____ in the County of _____ and State of _____. This is the same property conveyed to the seller by deed dated _____, 19_____, with _____ as grantor; the deed is recorded in the office of the Registrar of the City of _____, County of _____, in Book (or Reel) number _____, page _____. A _____-story, _____ family house has been constructed on this plot, and is covered by this contract.

This contract also covers personal property to be transferred for seller(s) to buyer(s) and included in the purchase price, as follows: _____. The seller(s) agree(s)/do(es) not agree to provide the buyer(s) with a bill of sale for this personal property. However, the following personal property is explicitly excluded from the sale: _____.

However, buyer(s) and seller(s) agree that no part of the purchase price will be allocated to the personal property. Furthermore, if the transaction described in this contract fails to close, the buyer(s) will have no obligation to purchase any of the personal property described above.

This contract also transfers any ownership and right the seller(s) may have in land lying in the bed of any street or highway now existing or to be built, in front of or adjoining the property described above up to the center line. If the seller (s) is/are entitled to any unpaid award for condemnation of his/her/their property described above, or for damage to the property described above caused by change in grade of any street or highway, this contract makes that unpaid award payable, instead, to the buyer(s).

The seller(s) agree(s) to transfer the property with the roof in good condition and the plumbing, heating, and electrical systems in working order. However, the property is sold in its present condition, subject to reasonable use and wear and tear from the contract date to the date of the closing.

4. (Purchase Price) The purchase price of the property will be $_____, payable as follows:

$ _____, already received, receipt of which is acknowledged

$ _____ payable on signing of this agreement, by check subject to collection

$ _____ by assumption of existing mortgage/deed of trust. A copy of this instrument is attached to this contract, and is hereby incorporated by reference.

$ by purchase money note by buyer(s) to seller(s)

$ _____ balance, payable at closing in cash/certified/cashier's check

The down payment will be held by the seller/seller's attorney/title company/ _____, the broker retained by the seller. Any person other than the seller who holds down payment funds does so merely as a stakeholder, and is free of any liability unless he or she misappropriates the funds or refuses to turn them over when so ordered by a court of competent jurisdiction. The stakeholder is directed to place the funds in a non-interest-bearing escrow account, until either the seller(s) deliver(s) the deed to the buyer(s) at closing, or the buyer(s) is/are entitled to a return of the down payment because a contingency provision of this contract has occurred or failed to occur, releasing the parties from their obligations.

5. (Title) The seller(s) agree(s) to give, and the buyer(s) to accept, good marketable title such as the _____ Title Company is willing to approve and insure under its standard title policy Form #_____. However, the sale of the property is subject to covenants and restrictions of record provided that they are not violated by existing improvements or their use, and provided that they do not render the title unmarketable. The property is also sold subject to any state of facts that would be disclosed by personal inspection and/or an accurate, current survey of the property.

6. (Deed to be Granted) The seller(s) agree(s) to deliver, at the closing, a quitclaim/bargain and sale with warranty against grantor's act/full covenant and warranty deed to the buyer(s) as sole owner/tenants in common/joint tenants/tenants by the entirety.

7. (Closing) The closing list to take place on or about _____, 19____, at the office of _____, located at _____, at a time to be set by the parties. Time is/is not of the essence in this contract.

8. (Risk of Loss) The seller retains the risk of loss or damage to the property until the closing.

9. (Conditions of Sale) The sale of the property is contingent on all of the conditions listed below. If any condition does not occur, the buyer(s) is (are) entitled to withdraw from the contract and is (are) entitled to return of the down payment. However, the seller(s) has (have) the right to cure any defect at his/her (their) expense before the first scheduled closing date; if the seller(s) do(es) this, the buyer(s) will be obligated under the contract as if the defect had not existed.

• Receipt of satisfactory reports on the condition of the house, its electrical, heating, plumbing, and mechanical systems, and freedom from termite infestation, rendered by licensed professionals qualified to make such reports; receipt of similar satisfactory reports on the property's drainage and grading, and on any septic tank located on the property.

• Receipt of a mortgage commitment on or before _____, 19____ in an amount of at least $ _____, with a fixed/variable interest rate of/ capped at not more than _____%. The buyer(s) agree(s) to make all reasonable efforts to secure such a commitment (e.g., by making prompt applications and cooperating with the lender's investigation process) and to provide the seller(s) with a copy of the commitment once it is received. The seller(s) has (have) the right to attempt to secure financing for the buyer (s); however, the buyer(s) is (are) not obligated to accept a purchase money mortgage in lieu of financing from a lending institution.

• The buyer(s) is (are) able to find a buyer for the home in which he/she (they) now live(s), at a price of at least $ _____ with a closing date not later than _____, 19____.

10. (Liquidated Damages for Breach) If the seller(s), acting in good faith, is (are) unable to convey good title to the property and thus the transaction is not consummated, the buyer (s) will be entitled to recover the down payment plus reasonable expenses, but no other damages. If the seller(s)' failure to convey good title is not in good faith, the buyer(s) is (are) entitled to return of the down payment plus interest, reasonable expenses, plus liquidated damages in the amount of $ _____ to compensate for loss of the benefit of the bargain.

If the buyer(s) fails to close under conditions not permitted by clause (9), above, the seller(s) is (are) entitled to retain the down payment, plus liquidated damages of $ _____ to compensate for loss of the benefit of the bargain.

11. (Closing Escrow) The seller(s) agree(s) to deposit 1% of the purchase price of the property in escrow. If the seller(s) have not vacated the property within ____ days after the closing, absent circumstances making it impossible to vacate the property, the seller(s) agree to pay the buyer (s) from said escrow the sum of $ _____ for every day after ____ days post-closing that the seller(s) remain on the property.

12. (Closing Adjustments) The following will be apportioned between buyer (s) and seller(s) as of midnight of the day before the closing:

• Fuel oil on hand

• rents payable to the seller (s) for portion of the property

• premiums on insurance policies that will be assigned to the buyer (s)

• taxes, water charges, and sewer rents. The seller (s) will make all reasonable efforts to obtain a water meter reading on or before _____, 19____.

Signed, _____ (Buyer) _____ (Seller)
_____ (Buyer) _____ (Seller)

7

FINANCING THE PROPERTY

The first contact this writer ever had with the term "mortgage" had elements of comedy and tragedy. A dastardly villain by the name of Silas Barnaby, waving a document in hand identified as a mortgage, threatened to foreclose on a little old lady who lived in a shoe unless the little old lady persuaded Little Bo Peep, an innocent damsel of astonishing beauty, to marry him.

To the rescue come the team of Stan Laurel and Oliver Hardy who, in typically blundering fashion, trick Barnaby into marrying Laurel disguised in a white wedding dress as Little Bo Peep. In the process, Ollie and Stanley take possession of the mortgage and save the shoe of the little old lady. Old Barnaby takes his revenge, naturally, and wild comedy follows in the movie, *The March of the Wooden Soldiers*.

That the movie has mortgage law more than a little distorted is obvious, and can be forgiven. It does, however, offer striking commentary on the importance of the document known as a mortgage to the health and well-being of the average home owner (whether the home is a house, condo, co-op, or shoe).

From approximately 1920 to the late 1970s, the "conventional" mortgage—20 to 30 year term, fixed interest rate, installment payments fully amortizing principle by end of term—reigned supreme. Then interest rates rose to unprecedented heights as did real estate prices. Many would-be buyers found they could not qualify for conventionals; and many banks found that they were holding too many mortgages yielding low interest while they had to woo depositors by paying high interest.

In response the banks created the raft of creative financing devices that greet buyers today. They include mortgages with adjustable interest rates, length of term, or both; short-term mortgages with a "balloon" (large balance remaining at term's end); arrangements in which the buyer agrees to share profits with the lender on resale of the home; agreements to pay modest sums in the first years of the mortgage term, larger payments thereafter.

Whatever form it takes, the modern mortgage, like its simpler counterpart in the past, is a crucial element in the real estate equation, for few buyers have the resources to tender the full purchase price in cash to the seller.

Mortgages are critical to the seller in the ordinary transaction as well. Unless he owns his home free and clear, he will either have to satisfy his own mortgage out of the sale proceeds or secure the lender's consent to allow the buyer to assume the mortgage. Moreover, if the seller is eager to accept a buyer's offer but the buyer experiences difficulty in qualifying for a lender's mortgage, or if prevailing mortgage rates are above the yield of competing investments, the seller may be willing to "take back" a purchase money mortgage for all or part of the sales price. According to a 1982 survey of real estate transactions in the southeastern United States, over 41 percent involved some degree of seller financing.

An interesting, and relatively new, take back mortgage concept sellers use is the so-called "wrap-around." The seller continues to make payments on his own mortgage after closing while taking back from the buyer a second mortgage usually at a higher interest rate.

PRACTICE TIP: If the homeowner has an FHA, VA, or conventional mortgage, and contemplates wrap-around financing, you should counsel him or her to investigate the Federal National Mortgage Association's Refinance/Resale Finance Program, which aims to harmonize FNMA's desire to avoid wrap-arounds (which perpetuate below-market interest rates) and the buyer's desire to achieve affordable financing. The program permits mortgages now held by FNMA to be refinanced in a single, below-market-rate, transaction.

For some mortgage holders today, the worst nightmare is payment shock: paying large monthly sums to service a mortgage at a high interest rate—and if such payments are capped, suffering the effects of "negative amortization." Negative amortization happens when monthly payments do not cover all the loan interest due and this interest shortage is automatically added to the debt, and interest may be charged on that amount.

PRACTICE TIP: If you are representing a buyer, be aware that standard American Land Title Association (ALTA) title insurance policies may not be sufficient for mortgages where negative amortization could occur. The problem arises because the standard policy excludes defects and liens arising subsequent to the date of the mortgage.

PRACTICE TIP: Incidentally, you should educate your buyer client to expect another kind of payment shock. Even if he achieves a conventional mortgage, monthly payments on it will not remain constant because each includes principal, interest, real estate tax, and insurance components. Insurance premiums will almost certainly increase over time; so will real estate taxes—at times dramatically so.

Dealing with the Legal Elements of a Mortgage Transaction

In essence, a mortgage is a conditional conveyance of realty from a mortgagor borrower to a mortgagee lender as security for the payment of a debt. It has two parts: (a) the signing of a promissory note (or bond) by the mortgagor, who thereby becomes personally liable to pay the note according to its terms; and (b) the execution of a mortgage deed, creating a security interest in the house and its land.

The mortgage deed is recorded, the note is not, because only the deed creates an interest in the property. The typical mortgage deed includes the mortgagor's covenants for title, and obligates the mortgagor to pay the indebtedness, plus the taxes, liens, and assessments on the property, to maintain the property in good repair, and to maintain adequate insurance for the mortgagee's benefit.

A deed of trust is conceptually a little different, but practically the same as, a mortgage. Under a deed of trust, the homeowner conveys the property to a third party who holds title in trust for the lender's benefit until the obligation under the deed is satisfied.

Deeds of trust are commonly used in Alaska, Arizona, California, Colorado, the District of Columbia, Missouri, Montana, Nevada, Tennessee, Texas, Virginia, and West Virginia; a related conveyance called a "security deed" is used in Georgia. Both deeds of trust and mortgages are used in Idaho, New Mexico, Oklahoma, and Washington—in these states, consult local practice and the desires of your client and the other parties to the transaction.

Mortgage Deed Checklist

A typical mortgage deed includes these provisions:

- identification of buyer and seller
- recital of amount of the mortgage debt, due date, rate of interest, and prepayment provisions

- identification of mortgage as first or second mortgage
- due-on-sale clause, or clause explaining conditions under which assumption is permitted
- foreclosure provisions, defining "default" and outlining the lender's remedies
- identification of property
- "habendum" clause, indicating borrower's right "to have and to hold" the property, subject to payment of mortgage installment payments and taxes, and subject to an obligation to keep the property in good repair
- signatures and acknowledgments.

The usual printed mortgage deed form is designed to be folded to fit a #10 envelope. On the "front" of the folded form are a caption identifying it as a mortgage; the names of borrower and lender; the date; and the name and address of the lender's attorney, so that the mortgage can be returned to the attorney once it has been recorded.

The "back" of the folded form contains a notice to the registrar or county clerk, applicable when the mortgage has been satisfied and the satisfaction recorded (and the mortgage sent back to the jubilant borrower).

The mortgage bond is a document indicating that the borrower is "held and firmly bound unto" the lender, and is obligated to make payments of a designated amount, on a designated schedule, to satisfy a specified debt and interest rate. The bond also contains default and any due-on-sale provisions.

Modern Mortgage Menu

Buyers' attorneys can perform a great service for their clients by becoming familiar with mortgage arrangements offered by local banks. They can give buyers a far more thorough (and objective) account of the real costs and consequences of a particular mortgage instrument than the loan officers are likely to do. Here are a few of the most popular mortgage arrangements and their legal implications:

Conventional Mortgage

A long-term (usually 15 to 30 years) amortized loan with a fixed interest rate and payment; applied first to the interest owed and then the balance to the principal amount over the term. As noted above, payments will not remain level throughout the term, because of the inevitable increases in real estate taxes and insurance.

Balloon Mortgage

A mortgage (usually short-term) whose last payment ("balloon payment") is much larger than the rest of the payments because the preceding payments will not fully amortize the amount of the loan by the time the final payment is due. The borrower must either pay this final "balloon" payment or refinance. Many borrowers lack the cash to make the balloon payment, and thus must take the risk that another loan will be unavailable, or that interest rates will have risen during the term of the balloon mortgage.

Wrap-Around Mortgage

A transaction in which the existing mortgage on the property is retained, and another loan usually at a higher interest rate is made on the property. The lender of the "wrap-around" loan (usually the seller of the property) makes the payments on the original mortgage, using the payments made by the buyer of the property. This arrangement makes it possible for the seller to continue making payments on a mortgage presumably secured at lower interest rates, while providing the buyer the financing needed to purchase the property.

FHA, VA Mortgage

The Federal Housing Administration (FHA) and Veterans' Administration (VA) do not provide mortgages. What they do is insure them, making it possible for banks to provide mortgages in transactions with low buyer down payments (actually none at all for VA mortgages). FHA and VA mortgages are subject to interest-rate ceilings, and buyers can be charged only one "point" (one percent of the selling price) in service charges, so these mortgages are not always popular with lenders, nor with sellers. If the buyer, for instance, has enough negotiating power and insists on an FHA or VA loan, the seller may have to pay points to the lender to induce it to make the loan. Thus, the seller will either have to raise the sales price to compensate, or accept a lower real return.

PRACTICE TIP: If you represent the buyer, he seeks an FHA-insured loan, and a contract of sale has yet to be signed, make the contract contingent on a statement from the FHA appraising the property at or above a specific value. This is because the maximum size of an FHA-insured loan depends on the property's assessed value.

Where a VA loan is involved, the contract of sale should make the closing contingent on the buyer's obtaining a preliminary loan commitment on or before a certain date, and final approval on or before another date. The contract should also provide that the buyer may withdraw from the transaction without penalty if the VA appraisal of the property is less than a specified amount.

Graduated Payment Mortgages (GPM)

This mortgage arrangement provides for small payments in the early years of the mortgage, larger payments later on. It can be useful for a young buyer who has good potential for higher earnings (and the ability to pay higher mortgage payments) later in the mortgage term. The department of Housing and Urban Development (HUD) has issued rules for FHA-insured GPMs, found at 12 USCA §1715z-10. The Federal Home Loan Banking Board (FHLBB) also has rules for GPMs issued by federally chartered savings and loan institutions; these rules are found at 12 CFR §545.6-3.

Growing Equity Mortgages (GEM)

Here, the buyer agrees to a payment schedule with lower initial payments, and later payments high enough to amortize the principal faster than under a conventional mortgage. This type of mortgage is controversial: some commentators feel that the GEM is no more advantageous to the buyer than refinancing or making prepayment if and when the buyer finds it convenient.

Shared Appreciation Mortgages (SAM)

The lender agrees to accept a below-market interest rate on condition that a determined percentage of the profit on eventual resale of the property is given to the lender. If you're interested in the conceptual problems created by this instrument, consult James T. Burnes' article, "The Shared Appreciation Mortgage—a Joint Venture, a Relationship Between Debtor and Creditor, or Both? in 12 *J. Real Estate Taxation* 195 (Spring 1985).

Purchase Money Mortgage (PMM)

The seller, at least nominally, provides part or all of the financing. "At least nominally, "because the seller is likely to resell the obligation rather than maintain it himself. The normal custom is for the seller's attorney to draw up the mortgage and note (or bond)—and for the buyer to pay for the legal services involved.

__PRACTICE TIP:__ If you have a PMM drafting assignment, you should consult standard forms such as New York's statutory short form of mortgage, and the comparable forms for other states (see, for example, MD. Art. 21 4-202). You should also check the standard forms issued by the various title companies.

In the very likely case that a resale of the obligation is desired, you should follow the Federal National Mortgage Association/Federal Home Loan Mortgage Corporation Uniform Instrument for the relevant state; that way, there will be no formal obstacles to a resale.

Adjustable Rate Mortgage (ARM) or Variable Rate Mortgage (VRM)

These instruments are popular with lenders because they require the borrower to assume the risk of interest rate changes. The mortgage contains an initial interest rate (which may be a below-market incentive rate designed to lure buyers), and a description of conditions under which the interest rate may change: for instance, the interest rate may be subject to recomputation after one, three or five years, and be set in conformity with an index chosen by the lender, such as the prime rate. Many ARMs protect the buyer against large increases in monthly payments by imposing a "cap": a maximum percentage that the interest rate can increase in a given adjustment and/or over the life of the loan.

It would appear that ARM rates would clash with low state usury ceilings. However, under 12 USCS §1735f-7, the provisions of any state constitution limiting "the rate or amount of interest, discount points, or other charges which may be charged, taken, received, or reserved by lenders" are preempted for any "federally related" first mortgage, so state usury laws do not affect ARMs.

Consumers are protected by the requirement that lenders abide by the Federal Home Loan Banking Board's consumer protection provisions dealing with balloons, prepayment penalties, late charges, refunds of unearned finance charges when the loan is prepaid, and 30-day notice of actions that could lead to foreclosure.

In this context, "federally related" means made by a lender whose loans are eligible for purchase by the Federal National Mortgage Association (FNMA—Fannie Mae), Government National Mortgage Association (GNMA—Ginnie Mae), or Federal Home Loan Mortgage Corporation (FHLMC—Freddie Mac); or made by a lender that is federally chartered, state-chartered but federally insured, or part of the Federal Reserve or Federal Home Loan Bank System.

More than half the mortgage loans made in the 1980s were resold on the secondary market (GNMA and the like), and most lending institutions fall into at least one of those categories, so nearly all first mortgages are, in fact, "federally related" and subject to usury law preemption and the FHLBB consumer protection provisions.

Note, however, that the states were given until the end of 1983 to opt out of this preemption of state regulation of usury. Twelve—Colorado, Georgia, Hawaii, Iowa, Kansas, Maine, Massachusetts, Minnesota, Nebraska, Nevada, South Dakota, and Wisconsin—took advantage of this option, and attorneys in these states should examine ARM documents with their state usury laws in mind.

Because of the complexity and potential for abuse in ARM transactions, they are heavily regulated. The Federal Home Loan Banking Board (FHLBB), which regulates federally chartered savings and loan banks has issued ARM rules that can be found at 12 CFR Part 545. Specifically, under these rules, interest rates are permitted to vary only according to the FHLBB's official index of cost of funds to FHLBB-insured institutions. (The index is published in the FHLBB Journal.)

Interest rates can be raised or lowered up to once a year, between .10 percent and .5 percent per year, with a maximum net increase of 2.5 percent over the life of the loan. The lender must decrease the interest rate when the FHLBB index drops, but rate increases are discretionary. (It's hard to imagine a permissible increase being passed up.)

Related rules for federally chartered banks have been promulgated by the Office of the Comptroller of the Currency at 12 CFR Part 29 and 23 CFR Part 29. The FHA's rules are found at 24 CFR Part 203. The Garn-St. Germain Depository Institutions Act of 1982, PL 97-302 §802 (b), moreover, authorizes housing creditors that are *not* federally regulated to "make, purchase, and enforce alternative mortgage transactions so long as the transactions are in conformity with the regulations issued by the Federal agencies."

Mortgage Disclosure

Even if the buyer is sophisticated enough to understand the legal consequences of the various mortgage types, he cannot make an intelligent selection unless he learns something about the actual costs of each type. Federal law requires lenders to disclose a great deal of information to borrowers—although the required disclosures can be so copious, and so confusing, that borrowers often find them virtually impossible to deal with.

The applicable law is the federal Truth in Lending Act (TILA), 15 U.S.C. 1601 et.seq. The Federal Reserve Board (FRB) has the power to promulgate regulations implementing TILA; and it has made lavish use of this power in Regulation Z (12 CFR Part 226). TILA and Reg. Z apply to all lenders, no matter how they are chartered. The FRB also issues simple standard disclosure forms— some examples are printed on pages 83-85.

Under TILA and Reg. Z credit is either "closed end" (the lender makes a single extension of credit, a mortgage, for example) or "open end" (repeated extensions for instance, a charge account or credit card). TILA and Reg. Z do not use the terms "principal," "interest," or "interest rate." Instead, they use concepts that are related, but different enough to cause an unholy degree of confusion.

All interest rates must be quoted in the form of Annual Percentage Rates (APRs), using prescribed methods of calculation so that consumers will not be deceived by manipulation of add-on and discount interest rates. The lender must disclose the "amount financed" rather than the principal of the loan, and must disclose "finance charges." As we'll see, finance charges include more than interest.

TILA Disclosures:

What information must the lender provide the borrower? Under 12 CFR §226.18, the lender must disclose information on the following checklist.

Lender Information Checklist

- lender's identity
- amount financed
- separate written itemization of amount financed, or a statement that borrower can request written itemization, or good-faith estimate of closing costs as required by RESPA (see pages 104-106)
- finance charge
- annual percentage rate (APR)
- if transaction involves a variable interest rate, either disclosure in a form approved by relevant federal bank regulatory agency (see page 88), or the following:
- • the circumstances under which the rate can increase
- • any limitations on the increase (for example, a "cap")
- • the effect of an increase
- • an example of the payment terms that would result from an increase
- number, amount, and timing of required payments
- total payments

Mortgage with Demand Feature Sample

Mortgage Savings and Loan Assoc.
Date: April 15, 1981
Account number 5782-39

Glenn Jones
700 Oak Drive
Little Creek, USA

ANNUAL PERCENTAGE RATE The cost of your credit as a yearly rate	FINANCE CHARGE The dollar amount the credit will cost you	Amount Financed The amount of credit provided to you or on your behalf	Total of Payments The amount you will have paid after you have made all payments as scheduled
14.85%	$156,551.54	$44,605.66	$201,157.20

Your payment will be

Numbers of Payments	Amount of Payments	When Payments are Due
360	$558.77	Monthly beginning 6/1/81

This obligation has a demand feature.

You may obtain property insurance from anyone you want that is acceptable to Mortgage Savings and Loan Assoc.. If you get the insurance from Mortgage Savings and Loan Assoc. you will pay $ __150 - 1 year__

Security: You are giving a security interest in:
☒ the goods or property being purchased.
☐ _____

Late Charge: If a payment is late, you will be charged $ __N/A__ __5__ % of the payment.

Prepayment: If you pay off early, you may have to pay a penalty.

Assumption: Someone buying your house may, subject to conditions, be allowed to assume the remainder of the mortgage on the original terms.

See your contract documents for any additional information about nonpayment, default, any required repayment in full before the scheduled date and prepayment refunds and penalties.

Valiable Rate Mortgage Sample

State Savings and Loan Assoc.

Ann Jones
600 Pine Lane
Little Creek, USA

Account number: 210802-47

ANNUAL PERCENTAGE RATE The cost of your credit as a yearly rate	FINANCE CHARGE The dollar amount the credit will cost you	Amount Financed The amount of credit provided to you or on your behalf	Total of Payments The amount you will have paid after you have made all payments as scheduled
15.07%	$157,155.20	$44,002—	$201,157.20

Your payment will be

Numbers of Payments	Amount of Payments	When Payments are Due
360	$558.77	Monthly beginning 6-1-81

Valiable Rate

The annual percentage rate may increase during the term of this transaction if the price rate of State Savings and Loan Assoc., increases. The rate may not increase more often than once a year, and may not increase by more than 1% annually. The interest rate will not increase above __19.75__ %. Any increase will take the form of higher payment amounts. If the interest rate increases by ____1____ % in __one year__ your regular payment would increase to $ __594.51__

Security: You are giving a security interest in the property being purchased.

Late Charge: If a payment is late, you will be charged 5% of the payment

Prepayment: If you pay early, ☒ may ☐ will not   have to pay a penalty.

Assumption: Someone buying your house may, subject to conditions, be allowed to assume the remainder of the mortgage on the original terms.

See your contract documents for any additional information about nonpayment, default, any required repayment in full before the scheduled date, and prepayment refunds and penalties.

Graduated Payment Mortgage Sample

Convenient Savings and Loan   Account number: 4862-68

Michael Jones
500 Walnut Court, Little Creek USA.

ANNUAL PERCENTAGE RATE The cost of your credit as a yearly rate	FINANCE CHARGE The dollar amount the credit will cost you	Amount Financed The amount of credit provided to you or on your behalf	Total of Payments The amount you will have paid after you have made all payments as scheduled
15.37%	$177,970.44	$43,777	$221,548.44

Your payment will be

Numbers of Payments	Amount of Payments	When Payments are Due
12	$ 446.62	monthly beginning 6/1/81
12	$ 479.67	" " 6/1/82
12	$ 515.11	" " 6/1/83
12	$ 553.13	" " 6/1/84
12	$ 593.91	" " 6/1/85
300	varying from $637.68 to $627.37	" " 6/1/86

Security: You are giving a security interest in the property being purchased.

Late charge: If a payment is late, you will be charged 5% of the payment.

Prepayment: If you pay off early, you
☒ may   ☐ will not   have to pay a penalty
☒ may   ☐ will not   be entitled to a refund of part of the finance charge

Assumption: Someone buying your home cannot assume the remainder of the mortgage on the original terms.

See your contract documents for any additional information about nonpayment, default, any required repayment in full before the scheduled date, and prepayment refunds and penalties.

- whether prepayment penalty will be imposed
- late payment charges
- whether required deposit (for example, a compensating balance—an amount that the borrower must maintain in an account with the lender) must be made; if it is, the lender must disclose that the required balance is not taken into account in computing the APR. However, "an escrow account for items such as taxes, insurance, or repairs" is not treated as a required deposit.

In general, lending institutions must make TILA disclosures before consummation of the loan transaction; "consummation" is defined as the creation of a contractual relationship between borrower and seller. If the transaction involves a residential mortgage and is covered by RESPA (see pages 104-106), the creditor "shall make good faith estimates of the disclosures required by §226.18 before consummation, or shall deliver or place them in the mail not later than three business days after the creditor receives the consumer's written application, whichever is earlier." (12 CFR §226.19 (a).)

Conditions being what they are, three business days after the application is almost inevitably weeks or months before loan consummation. Remember that a formal (and expensive) application, not a mere inquiry about mortgage terms, triggers the disclosure.

The Finance Charge

The concept of finance charge is a sophisticated one, and confuses many clients, but is not all that difficult to understand or explain. The finance charge is interest, plus certain other amounts a lending institution charges a credit consumer.

More specifically, the finance charge is defined to include "service, transaction, activity, and carrying charges", and "points, loan fees, assumption fees, finder's fees, and similar charges," in addition to interest. Nominally, premiums for credit insurance must be included in the finance charge. However, the lender does not have to include them if it discloses that the insurance is optional, and also that the borrower can choose his own insurance carrier rather than obtaining the insurance from the lender. (12 CFR §226.4 (b).)

However, the definition of the finance charge does not include seller's points (12 CFR §226.4 (c)(5)). As you'll recall, seller's points are common in FHA and VA-insured transactions, because buyer's points are limited; the seller must frequently pay points to make the transaction attractive to the lender.

Certain fees do not have to be reported as part of the finance charge if they are "bona fide and reasonable in amount":

- fees for title examination, abstract of title, title insurance, property survey, and similar purposes
- fees for preparing deeds, mortgages, and related documents
- fees for appraisals, notarization, or credit reports

- amounts that must be paid into escrow, but are not otherwise included in the finance charge (12 CFR §226.4 (c)(7).

Thus, the borrower may have to spend quite a bit of money for items that are not considered part of the finance charge for TILA purposes, and the borrower will be in a lot of trouble if he relies only on TILA for an accurate idea of the financial consequences of a mortgage loan.

The Federal Reserve System has issued some official staff interpretations (found on pp. 737-8 of the CFR volume containing Regulation Z) which are helpful in clearing up the potentially confusing language related to the finance charge concept. One interpretation is that TILA disclosures are not required in transactions involving the purchase of a three- or more family house, even if it is owner-occupied (because this is considered a business transaction, not personal, household, or family credit).

Even the purchase of a two-family house may be treated as a transaction for business purposes, depending on the specific fact situation. In this case, you will have to instruct your buyer client about matters that would otherwise be disclosed by the lender under TILA.

Lenders do not have to include "application fees" in their finance charge. An application fee in this contract is defined as "a charge to recover the costs associated with processing applications for credit," and may include services such as credit reports, credit investigations, and appraisals. "The creditor is free to impose the fee in only certain of its loan programs, such as mortgage loans. However, if the fee is to be excluded from the finance charge under §226.4(c)(1), it must be charged to all applicants, not just to applicants who are approved or who actually receive credit."

The lender need not incur costs for the application fee to be excludible from disclosure of the finance charge: such fees are excluded from the finance charge "even if the services for which the fees are imposed are performed by the creditor's employees rather than by a third party. In addition, credit report fees include not only the cost of the report itself, but also the cost of verifying information in the report."

"A charge for a lawyer's attendance at the closing or a charge for conducting the closing (for example, by a title company) is excluded from the finance charge if the charge is primarily for services related to items listed in §226.4 (c)(7) (for example, reviewing or completing documents), even if other incidental services, such as explaining various documents or disbursing funds for the parties, are performed."

The vexed question of *seller's* points is also taken up by the Federal Reserve Board. "The seller's points mentioned in §226.4 (c)(5) include any charges imposed by the creditor upon the non-creditor seller of property for providing credit to the buyer or for providing credit on certain terms. These charges are excluded from the finance charge even if they are passed on to the buyer, for example, in the form of a higher sales price. Seller's points are frequently involved in real estate transactions guaranteed or insured by governmental agencies. A "commitment fee" paid by a non-creditor seller (such as a real estate developer) to the creditor should be treated as seller's points. Buyer's points (that is, points charged to the buyer by the creditor), however, are finance charges."

If a noncreditor seller pays mortgage insurance premiums or other charges for the borrower (a common practice for real estate developers who advertise "no closing costs" as an incentive), the creditor can treat these payments as seller's points, and need not include them in the finance charge.

ARM Disclosure

For adjustable rate mortgages, various federal bank-chartering agencies enter the scene, and alternate disclosure forms may be permitted. The Federal Reserve Board has special rules for disclosure of discounted ARMS (12 CFR §226.18 (e)). A discounted ARM is a variable-rate loan whose initial rate (or rates) is set below market rate to attract buyers, rather than by the index or formula used to compute later adjustments in the rate. An ARM is not considered "discounted" if its initial low rate is set before consummation and then must be adjusted at the time of consummation on the basis of the index or formula used for later adjustments because interest rates or other adjustment factors have changed.

Under the FRB's rules for discounted ARMs, the APR quoted for the loan must be a composite based on the initial rate for as long as it applies (for example, the first year) and the rate that would apply to the rest of the term, using the index or formula used at consummation. The effect of multiple rates must be reflected in the disclosure of the finance charge, number of payments, and the payment schedule as well. The disclosures must also reflect any cap that would keep the initial rate from changing to the rates set under the index.

The Federal Home Loan Banking Board (again, which regulates federally chartered savings and loans banks) has issued its own rules on ARMS, which replace the TILA rules for ARMs issued by savings and loan institutions. Under 12 CFR §545.32, these rules apply to mortgages on one-four family residences. The index the banks use to adjust interest rates must be verifiable, and the index must not be within the control of the institution making the loan. Moreover, borrowers must be given the right to make prepayments, without penalty, within 90 days of a notice of adjustment.

The FHLBB's rules for ARM disclosure (12 CFR §545.33) require the lender to disclose:

- term of contract
- initial interest rate (if this is known when the disclosures are made; it might not be, if interest rates are volatile and the length of time between application and consummation is considerable)
- amount of initial monthly payments
- explanation of how lender establishes amortization schedule
- index used to adjust rates
- how adjustments can be made

- amount and type of notice that will be given of adjustments
- descriptions of any contingencies that could lead to acceleration of loan balance or forced sale of home
- if there is a balloon feature, disclosure of the balloon and a statement that the lender is not obligated to refinance the loan when the balloon comes due
- disclosure of provisions relating to escrow and prepayment
- examples of how various factors interrelate over time (for example, possible monthly payments based on various interest-rate assumptions).

For *national banks*, the Office of the Comptroller of the Currency has issued regulations (23 CFR §29.1) with similar rules about indexes used to adjust the rate. However, under these regulations the disclosure required is even more elaborate than the TILA rules. The OCC, for example, addresses the special problems of "rollover" mortgages (short-term mortgages made with the obvious intention of refinancing) by requiring additional disclosure.

Mortgage Disclosure Case Law:

Even with the regulation just described, a number of points remain unclear, and it helps to turn to the case law and see how they have been adjudicated.

Timing requirements are addressed by *Postow v. OBA Federal S&L*, 627 F2d 1370 (1st Cir. 1980), which holds that disclosures must be accomplished before a loan commitment is secured by a borrower paying a non refundable "stand-by" fee—the lender can't wait until both the borrower and the lender have signed the mortgage note to consider the deal "consummated." Under this analysis, credit is extended as soon as the lender is obligated to lend, and the borrower has paid a fee that will be forfeited if he fails to borrow.

TILA and Regulation Z place obligations on lenders—what about non-lenders who are approached for information?

Wyatt v. Union Mortgage Co., 157 Cal.Rptr. 392, 598 P.2d 45 (1979) finds that it is a question for the jury whether a mortgage loan broker (a "matchmaker" between lending institutions and would-be borrowers) and affiliated corporations can be liable under a civil conspiracy theory for providing incomplete and materially misleading answers to questions about interest rates, late payment charges, and balloon payments. The court considered agency law (because the mortgage broker is retained as the buyer's agent) and the duties imposed on a state-licensed person.

The question of what should be disclosed as a finance charge has occupied many courts, for example:

- fees for recording assignments of mortgages don't belong in the finance charge—they should be disclosed either as "recording fees" or in a miscellaneous category: *Schroder v. Suburban Coastal Corp.*, 550 F.Supp. 377 (SD Fla. 1982).

- delinquency charges assessed only against the late payment (not the entire balance) need not be disclosed in the finance charge; and the FRB's regulation, mandating disclosure of attorney fees and other foreclosure costs only if they are automatically imposed, not if they are conditioned on the actual employment of an attorney, is reasonable: *Vega v. First Federal S&L of Detroit*, 433 F.Supp. 424 (ED Mich. 1977).

It is clear that 12 CFR §226.8(e)(2) specifically excludes escrow accounts from the definition of "required deposit balances" that must be disclosed. What about the interest on tax and insurance escrow amounts—must it be disclosed? *Moore v. Great Western S&L*, 513 F.2d 688 (9th Cir. 1975) says no, finding this amount to be neither a finance charge separately paid nor a required deposit balance.

Due-on-Sale Clauses

Unless the buyer can (and will) pay cash and unless the house to be sold is mortgage free, there are three main conceptual approaches to what can happen at closing. Either seller's mortgage continues in force, and another mortgage is "wrapped" around it; buyer assumes the seller's mortgage; or obtains financing independent of seller's mortgage and seller satisfies his own mortgage out of the proceeds of the sale.

Most mortgages are drafted to include a "due-on-sale" clause permitting the lender to accelerate the maturity of the loan when the property is sold. When interest rates are rising, lenders have an understandable incentive to replace the old, low-rate mortgages in their portfolios with mortgages at market rates. Therefore, they are very likely to refuse their consent to mortgage assumption and invoke the Due-on-Sale clause.

As interest rates began their ascent in the late seventies and early eighties, a number of state courts (for example, California, in *Wellenkamp v. Bank of America*, 21 Cal.3d 943, 148 Cal.Rptr. 379, 582 P.2d 970 (1978)) ruled that due-on-sale clauses were invalid as restraints on alienation if the lender accelerated maturity of the loan for any reason other than impairment of its security. *West v. Buffo*, 139 Cal. 3d 93, 188 Cal.Rptr. 535 (1983) applies *Wellenkamp* to purchase money mortgages—as we'll see, *Wellenkamp* is no longer good law, but this case is useful for extending the due-on-sale analysis to PMMs.

Federal legislators and regulators, however, were concerned by the plight of the savings and loan institutions which were threatened by failure because they were "borrowing short" (offering depositors high interest rates to attract deposits) and "lending long" (holding a portfolio of 20- and 30-year low-interest mortgages). Under the Garn-St. Germain Depository Institutions Act (relevant provisions at 12 USCA §1701j-3) and FHLBB regulations (12 CFR §545.8-3(f)) lenders were specifically authorized to enter into and enforce due-on-sale clauses in real property loans, notwithstanding contrary provisions in state laws or constitutions, and state court decisions. They were also exempted from FHLBB restrictions on balloon payments.

The Act defines a due-on-sale clause as a contract provision that gives the lender the option to declare the mortgage principal due and payable if all or part of the property (or an interest in the property) is sold or transferred without prior written consent of the lender. Lenders are "encouraged" to allow assumption at the seller's mortgage rate or at a rate between the seller's and the market rate, but they are not required to do so.

The Office of the Comptroller of the Currency has issued due-on-sale regulations for national banks (12 CFR §30.1). The bank must permit assumption on the same terms as the original loan, except that it may increase the interest rate to a "blended" rate (between the original rate and contemporary market rates) and change the payments to reflect this. The lender can accelerate if the buyer does not meet the lender's credit standards, or fails, fifteen days after the lender's request, to provide credit information.

In *Fidelity Federal S&L v. de la Cuesta*, 458 US 141 (1982), the Supreme Court upheld the Garn-St Germain Depository Act and FHLBB regulations, finding that the pervasiveness of federal regulation of mortgage lending shows a Congressional intent to preempt contrary state regulation.

Haugen v. Western Federal S&L, 649 P.2d 323 (Co. 1982) reads *de la Cuesta* to say that the FHLBB regulations preempt all state regulation on mortgage assumptions, including the state law at bar that limited rate increases on assumption to one percent. *Malouff v. Midland Federal S&L,* 509 P.2d 1240 (Co. 1973); *Lindenberg v. First Federal S&L,* 691 F.2d 974 (11th Cir. 1982). *Torgerson-Forstrom H.I. of Wilmar, Inc. v. Olmstead Fedl'l S&L,* 339 NW2d 901 (Minn. 1983) interpret a due-on-sale clause saying "consent [to assumption] shall not be unreasonably withheld" to permit the lender to refuse for reasons other than impairment of its security—and therefore the lender can demand a "reasonable" rate increase as a condition of its consent.

However, the federal law provides that exercise of the due-on-sale clause is exclusively governed by the terms of the loan contract. *Morse v. City Federal S&L,* 567 F.Supp. 699 (SD Fla. 1983) concerns a somewhat improvidently drafted mortgage that gave the lender the right to accelerate if the property was transferred without the lender's written consent and without "assumption in the regular form of law." The buyer did assume the mortgage, and the court held that the lender had no right to accelerate, because the terms of the mortgage had been complied with. Even if the lender had had the right to accelerate, the *Morse* court found that he would have been precluded from increasing the interest rate by the terms of the contract.

Where the mortgage allowed the lender either to accelerate maturity or consent to assumption of the mortgage with a rate increase of up to two percent, the lender was not permitted to change the maturity of the loan when it was assumed. Once consent to assumption is given, acceleration is no longer an option for the lender: *United Savings Bank Mut. v. Zandol*, 70 Or.App. 239, 689 P.2d 335 (1984).

Note, that, even where the lender violates the provisions of the Garn-St. Germain Act with regard to due-on-sale clauses, there is no private right of action for the mortgagor: *Dupuis v. Yorkville Federal S&L*, 589 F.Supp. 820 (SDNY 1984).

Prepayment Penalties

It's not uncommon for a mortgage to be written so that a penalty is required if part or all of the principal is prepaid—either because the home has been sold, or because the homeowner has access to cash or refinancing. The seller's problem is that when interest rates are declining, the lender is unlikely to exercise the due-on-sale clause (because the mortgage probably has an above-market rate)—but may still require the prepayment penalty. In California, for example, in 1983 the median assumed loan was $65,000, with a median penalty of $4,000.

The FHLBB permits prepayment of 20 percent of the balance in any year without penalty, limits prepayment penalties on the remainder to six months' interest on the balance beyond the first 20 percent (12 CFR §545.6-12(b)), and forbids prepayment penalties when a due-on-sale clause is exercised (12 CFR §591.5(a)). For federally related first mortgages, all prepayment penalties are forbidden, and the right to prepay must be disclosed in type larger than that used for the body of the mortgage: 12CFR §490.4(d).

There are also state laws on prepayment penalties. Pennsylvania's Title §41 405 forbids prepayment penalties altogether; Illinois' chapter 74 §4(2)(c) forbids them in mortgages with an interest rate over eight percent, which means nearly all mortgages. Michigan (§438.31C), Massachusetts (Chapter 183 54), and New Jersey (§46:10B-2) forbid prepayment penalties after the third year of a mortgage; Wisconsin (§138.052(2)(a)) forbids them after five years. Although federal law preempts state regulation of mortgage interest rates, it does not preempt limitations on "prepayment charges, attorneys' fees, late charges or other provisions designed to protect borrowers": 12 CFR §590.3(c).

However, the office of the Comptroller of the Currency does permit *national banks* offering or purchasing adjustable-rate mortgages to charge prepayment penalties despite state-law limitations. Prepayments, for this purpose, are defined to exclude payments made to avoid or reduce negative amortization, and payments computed according to the indexing rules given in the mortgage instrument: 12 CFR §29.6.

"Redlining" and Application Delays

No matter how willing the buyer and seller are, no matter how much the buyer knows about the mortgage terms offered to him or her, problems can still arise. This chapter concludes with hints about coping with some of the most common problems.

Redlining:

Traditionally, lenders have identified some neighborhoods (usually minority and/or slum areas) as "bad risks", and refused to write mortgages for homes in those areas no matter how high the applicants' incomes and credit ratings were.

This practice of "redlining" has been attacked by the Community Reinvestment Act of 1977 (12 USCS §2901) and the OCC regulations at 12 CFR Part 25. Under these regulations, decisions about national banks' charters, branching, and mergers will be made based in part on their record in meeting the credit needs of the areas in which their branches are located. Banks must post statements showing their records in making local loans, and must make files of comments from the public available to the public. The comments relate to the bank's performance in placing loans in the community—so encourage your clients to place any complaints they have in this regard on the record.

Of course it takes more than legislation to end prejudice, but this statute and its implementing regulations are a useful step forward.

Application Delays:

Most contracts of sale are drafted to be contingent on the buyer's securing financing on specified terms within a four- to seven-week period. But if the buyer starts shopping for a mortgage after signing a contract of sale, he or she will be hard pressed indeed to obtain information, make a selection, make an application, and have it processed in time for the scheduled closing. Assuming the contract language does not cover delays, the seller may agree to an adjournment of the closing if the buyer needs more time—but if he is concerned about the closing on another house, or begins to feel that he could have found other buyers at a higher price, he may insist either on performance on the original terms or cancellation of the contract. Or, the contract may require the buyer to pay a penalty for the delays.

The buyer's lawyer can be very effective in educating the buyer, about financing (thus reducing the amount of information the buyer must coax from potential lenders, and permitting him or her to apply more efficiently by, for instance, assembling and delivering evidence of income levels and other forms of credit-worthiness at the initial contact with the bank, so that the application can be completed in full at once). *PRACTICE TIP: You can help your clients a great deal by keeping current on the terms offered by local banks, and perhaps by maintaining relationships with local bankers that will encourage the mortgage officer to speed your client's application "through the pipeline." Moreover, you can and should call frequently to check on the progress of the application, and back up the calls with summary letters.*

Delays in mortgage applications, however, are a fact of modern life. The best approach is to draft sales contracts and set closing dates in light of these delays.

Example: What I suggest to many of my clients is to confirm in writing information they receive from a lender about their applications. I set forth here in full an excellent letter written on my advice by one of my clients to a Long Island, New York, mortgage broker.

We have been advised by our attorney to submit a written understanding of our mortgage application terms with the _____ Corporation to avoid any misunderstandings or discrepancies at closing.

We have remitted one thousand four hundred dollars ($1,400) which represents a one-point origination fee (based on a $110,000 mortgage) of $1,100 to lock in the rate at a maximum of 8.25 percent and a $300 application fee. We have applied for a three-year adjustable mortgage at the aforementioned rate with a cap of 1.5 percent per three-year period and a maximum lifetime ceiling of 12.75 percent. It is our understanding that this rate will be adjusted based on three-year U.S. Treasury Bills.

Within the next five to seven days, we will receive a confirmation of the application described above and a good faith estimate of our anticipated closing costs. These will include 2.5 points and the customary closing costs approximated below:

Attorney Fee: $500

Title Insurance: $595

New York State Mortgage Tax: $800

Recording Fees: $50

Flood Search: $10

Points: $2750

Initial Mortgage Payment: $826.10

Taxes: $1700

Homeowner's Insurance: $30

(Survey has been provided and our attorney will do title search).

It is our understanding that the _____ Corporation will give a written confirmation that the total points will be 3.5 (1 at application and 2.5 at closing) and that there are no other fees other than those approximated above.

Thank you for your assistance with our mortgage application. Please notify us immediately if any of the information contained here is erroneous. Sincerely.

Couldn't have written a better letter myself!

8

THE CLOSING

What we traditionally know as the "closing" is the final event of the typical real estate transaction. It is when the seller transfers the deed to the buyer for the purchase price contracted for weeks earlier, and the two—and, in many states, a bank, and a title company, and a broker, and two attorneys—finish up all other business connected with the sales contract. Actually, there are two closings in most deals, the title closing just described, and the loan closing between buyer and bank, both of which occur at the same time and in the same place.

Closings often have the quality of celebrations because everyone in attendance comes away with something valuable: the seller walks off with a sizable chunk of cash, the buyer with a deed and keys to a new home, the bank with a nice mortgage investment, the broker with a fat commission, the title company with a service fee, and the attorneys with monies owed to them.

Whether the closing ends in smiles and handshakes or on a much less successful note—whether it runs like clockwork or *A Clockwork Orange*—pretty much depends on how well the players have prepared for the big event, particularly the attorneys involved. **_PRACTICE TIP:_** *You can virtually assure a successful outcome with proper rehearsal.* As the closing date approaches, contact the bank, title company, your client, and the other attorney and review every aspect of the closing, including the final breakdown of figures and distribution of monies. Prepare a checklist to assist you in this regard, and draft a closing statement to reflect these figures and monies. On the basis of this statement, you should explain all debits and credits to be expected by your client—especially significant for a buyer client who must know how much money he needs to close.

Immediately before the closing, sort out the material in your file so that you can quickly produce only those documents relevant for the meeting. Few things in your professional life will be more embarrassing than a situation in which you fumble or misplace a document or otherwise appear disorganized at the closing table. Few things in your professional life will be more unforgiveable than if, after all the players are assembled, the closing founders because you forgot to produce a document or perform some act absolutely essential for the closing to occur—such as failing to have your buyer client obtain homeowner's insurance, evidence of which is almost always required by a lending institution as a condition for the transfer of mortgage funds. Sometimes no matter how well you prepare, you just can't win.

EXAMPLE: A seller's attorney promised a colleague of mine, representing a buyer, that the seller would deliver a certificate of occupancy on the property by closing. The seller's attorney had claimed that it could not be delivered sooner because the seller had "misplaced it."

Why was the document necessary for the buyer? In the course of his ownership of the property, the seller had remodeled his basement and built three separate offices for a business he had decided to run. The certificate would testify that (a) the alterations had complied with public health and building codes, and (b) they had been taken into account in the real estate tax base the seller had represented that the buyer would assume with the transfer of ownership. This is obviously an important matter.

At closing, my colleague requested the certificate. The seller's attorney stated that his client had been unable to locate it—never having mentioned to my colleague in any of the phone conversations immediately preceding the closing that the certificate would not be available.

The imperfect solution decided upon was that part of the purchase price would be placed in escrow by the seller's attorney until such time as the certificate was conveyed to the buyer.

It never was: The seller had never obtained the certificate in the first instance; the buyer was forced to apply for a certificate and when he did so saw his real estate taxes skyrocket; and my colleague brought an action against the seller and his attorney for fraud.

Closing practice around the country is very idiosyncratic, varying not only from state to state but in various parts of certain states as well.

Conference Closing

So-called "conference closings" bring together buyer, seller, their attorneys, lender and title company, and sometimes other participants, and are either the general rule or an alternative in 33 states.

Out of this group, the lender orchestrates the closing in North Dakota; the lender and title company in Ohio; and the title company in New York, Oklahoma, and Pennsylvania.

Escrow Closings

"Escrow closings" are those generally carried out by an escrow agent such as a title company, a specialized escrow company, or an attorney, who holds documents and check until the agent is satisfied that the transaction is complete and in proper form. They are the rule or frequent in Alaska, Arizona, Arkansas, California, Colorado, the District of Columbia, Hawaii, Idaho, Illinois, Indiana, Kansas, Missouri, Nevada, southern New Jersey, New Mexico, Oregon, Utah, Washington, and Wisconsin.

Even the customary place for the closing is subject to geographical variations. In the Midwest, and parts of the East (for example, New York), the usual place is the lender's office, but the office of the title company is gaining popularity. In the Western states, the specialized escrow or title company's office is the popular site; in many sections of the East, the office of one of the attorneys is more common. (Of course, the parties may agree to any location if the conventional one is inconvenient for them.)

Despite local variations, the basic tasks of the closing are uniform. Before the property changes hands, the seller's title must be reviewed. If there are still any defects in title, they must either be cured; the buyer must accept the property with the defects; or the transaction must be cancelled. It must be determined whether both parties have complied with the contract of sale (for example, seller is delivering the property in the promised condition); if not either a cure must take place or remedies must be applied. The closing costs on the property must be apportioned between the parties (determined by local custom and negotiation) and closing costs for the mortgage must be recited by the lender to the buyer (see pages 103 and 104). Documents such as deeds, mortgages, and mortgage notes must be reviewed and then signed in preparation for recording. Items such as real estate taxes and fuel on hand must be factored into the calculation of how much money must change hands. Finally, in the usual transaction, the buyer takes possession of the deed and property, the seller the balance of the sales proceeds (i.e. purchase price less any down payment).

PRACTICE TIP: *Note that the Tax Code of 1986 adds a new requirement: that the person or entity "responsible for closing the transaction" submit an information return to the Treasury. The Code contains a priority listing of parties responsible for the return—starting* *with the title company, but including the attorney "handling the settlement" if no title company is involved.*

Preparing for the Closing: Checklist for the Buyer's Lawyer

Note that, whether there will be a conference or escrow closing, and whichever side you represent, you must be familiar with all the tasks of the closing, and you must check to see that they're performed on schedule. A reminder by you to a dilatory opposing attorney may make the difference between a smooth closing on schedule and an inconvenient and expensive delay, or even the termination of the transaction.

- If the closing date is not specified in the contract of sale, set a closing date in consultation with your client, the seller and seller's attorney, and the lender, based on the typical mortgage application period and the title company's estimate of how long it will take to search the title and issue the necessary policy. Be sure the closing date is realistic—even if the buyer had a lending institution in mind before making an offer on the house, the application process can take as much as eight or more weeks.

- Make a note of the expiration date for the mortgage commitment—it could expire before the closing, and an extension will be required.

- Make sure that your client has fully performed his obligations under the contract.

- If the property is newly constructed, review the "punch list" (list of tasks to be completed by the builder); make sure your client has received everything for which he has contracted. Also find out if the HOW (Home Owner's Warranty) program is available to your clients. Under this program, certain defects of newly built homes will be repaired without charge to the homeowner during the period the warranty is in effect.

- Make sure that information about water and sewer bills, real estate taxes, and fuel on hand is available in time to inform the client of possible monies that must be exchanged at closing.

- If necessary, arrange for a supplemental title search to cover the "gap" period between the date of the first search and the closing.

- If the buyer is to assume the mortgage, make sure the seller obtains the lender's consent in time for the scheduled closing date.

- Review the "exceptions sheet" on the title report: are there any defects in title? What can be done about them? Remember that some title/defects will not preclude the lender or the buyer from closing the transaction, but which can be inconvenient for the buyer. For instance, there may be a utility easement at a point where the buyer would like to build an extension to the house. Are there any outstanding judgments against the seller (or any satisfied judgments unrefuted by the records)? any *lis pendens* (pending suit) against the property?

- The buyer's attorney often renders an opinion on the validity of title, based on the "abstract" (or summary) of title and the abstractor's certificate of what records have been examined. It may be necessary to examine records (for example, zoning UCC-1 fillings, building code violations) that the abstractor did not examine. Your opinion states who is the holder of record title on the last date covered; what, if anything, is wrong with the title, and how the defects can be corrected.

- When the deed is submitted to you for review, make sure it conforms both to local practice and the sales contract; make sure that, if husband and wife sellers are involved, both have joined in the conveyance. If there is anything unconventional about the form of the deed, it is good practice to have the lender "sign off" on it in advance, to avoid protests and possible delays at closing.

- If your state taxes homestead property at a lower rate, make sure your client indicates the homestead nature of the property to the appropriate taxing authorities. (A "homestead" is roughly equivalent to a principal residence, a "family home"; in addition to lower tax rates, a homestead may be entitled to protection against certain creditors.)

- Even if the lender's documents do not include an amortization schedule for the mortgage, try to obtain one—it will make your client's life much easier when tax time rolls around.

- If the seller has agreed to assign his homeowner's insurance policies to the buyer, find out when the property was last appraised—the seller's coverage may be inadequate to satisfy the mortgage's coinsurance clause. Find out if the buyer can simply estimate the additional coverage required, or if a new appraisal will be needed.

It's also important to check to see that the assignment really does take place; or, if the lender insists that the seller's policy be replaced, that a new policy is in fact obtained. In *Hardcastle v. Greenwood S&L*, 9 Wash.App. 884, 516 P.2d 228 (1973), the lender agreed to secure replacement insurance coverage for the buyer. The court held that the mortgagee becomes the mortgagor's agent in this situation, and can be held liable if it is negligent in failing to tell the mortgagor that it couldn't acquire the coverage originally contemplated, and had not bothered to secure substitute coverage. Although, in this case, the mortgagee was estopped from foreclosing after the (uninsured) premises were damaged by fire, and was ordered to pay damages to the mortgagor, it's still better to avoid using the mortgagee to accomplish the necessary insurance.

The mortgagee will not be treated as the mortgagor's agent in all situations. In *Schell v. Knickelbein*, 77 Wis.2d 344, 252 N.W.2d 921 (1977), the court denied recovery to the widow of a person killed by a homeowner's dog in her suit against the savings and loan institution that allegedly failed to procure homeowner's insurance for the mortgagors.

- If the area is prone to flooding, investigate the possible need for federal flood insurance. It's important for your client to take steps to get any necessary insurance, not wait for the lender to suggest it.

Neither the Federal Flood District Protection Act of 1973 nor the National Flood Insurance Act creates an implied federal right of action against a lender who does not inform the borrower of the availability of, or need for, federal flood insurance: *Hofbauer v. Northwestern National Bank of Rochester*, 700 F.2d 1197 (8th Cir. 1983). *Hofbauer* finds that there may be a common-law negligence claim against the lender, but that it should be pursued in state, not federal court. Once again, a few words from the attorney can avert the problem.

- Discuss the pros and cons of mortgage life insurance (although it is more expensive than conventional life insurance, and may not be necessary if your client has adequate estate assets to pay the mortgage after his or her death, it can be very useful for poor credit risk buyers with limited assets and insurance. If the client chooses to carry such coverage, make sure it is in fact obtained.

Burgess v. Charlottesville S&L, 349 F.Supp. 133 (W.D. VA. 1972) holds that, even where borrowers indicate to a bank providing a Truth in Lending (TILA) disclosure statement that they want credit life insurance, the bank is not negligent if it fails either to obtain the insurance or tell the borrowers that they are not covered. Under the Burgess analysis, borrowers are held responsible for knowing that an oral request is not enough to create a contract of insurance, and that they have to make an application and pay premiums. But it's all too easy for buyers to forget this detail in the press of other decisions to be made and steps to be taken. Again, the lawyer can and should educate them and make sure they follow through on their decision.

- If the seller is an heir or devisee, make sure that this status has been proved, and that the estate has been wound up properly (payment of all transfer taxes and debts; distribution of legacies)—otherwise, taxing authorities, creditors, or other beneficiaries or would-be beneficiaries could challenge the sale.

- Acquire a bill of sale, if necessary, for any personal property included in the sale (for example, carpeting, draperies, washer-dryer).

- If the property has been surveyed recently, obtain an affidavit from the seller that there have been no changes since the date of that survey.

- Notify the taxing authorities of the change in the party to be billed. Make sure your clients understand the tax schedule, so they can make sure the changeover has been make.

- Compute adjustments and prorations. Make sure your client understands how much money he must pay at the closing; to whom; and in what form (for example, whether certified checks will be required).

Preparing for the Closing: Checklist for the Seller's Lawyer

The seller's lawyer's major responsibilities with respect to the closing are to cope with the seller's existing mortgage (whether by satisfaction or assumption), to draft any purchase money mortgage (PMM) involved in the transaction, and to draft the deed and prepare the transfer tax return.

- Contact the mortgagee holding seller's mortgage for a report on the amounts already paid off on that mortgage, payments scheduled between the time of your request and closing, and balance operating as a lien as of the closing date if all payments are made on time. Secure a satisfaction letter or "sat" from the mortgagee specifying these matters. The mortgagee's attorney may charge a fee for preparing it; the title company will usually charge for picking it up at the closing and thereafter recording it.

EXAMPLE: A satisfaction statement I reviewed at a recent closing contained the following information: date of statement, mortgage number, mortgagor name, property address, principal balance of mortgage (as of sat date), interest projection from sat date to closing date, accumulated late charges, prepayment penalty, satisfaction fee (preparation of satisfaction by bank attorney), per diem rate (to be applied if closing takes place after initially scheduled closing date), present escrow balance (to be returned upon payment of mortgage), and "total to satisfy"—based on all of the preceding calculations.

- If the buyer is assuming the seller's mortgage, make sure the mortgagee provides written evidence of consent well before the scheduled closing date (an "estoppel letter," permitting buyer to take title subject to the mortgage).
- Prepare the bond and mortgage for any PMM. Make sure to bill the buyer for these services, which is traditional.
- Prepare the deed in appropriate form (for example, use a fiduciary deed if the seller is an estate; signatures to be witnessed; property to be described by address, block and lot number, or both; names to be printed or typed beneath signatures; your own name as drafter to be included). Because printed form deeds are usually used, it is especially important to make sure that the correct form is selected (for example, don't use a corporate deed form where the grantor is an individual).

Don't be in too much of a hurry—although it is possible to obtain revenue tax stamps before the closing, don't affix them; and don't have the original of the deed executed before the closing, just in case there is a problem.

If the state has a compulsory or voluntary Torrens system, that is, one in which the condition of the title can easily be discovered without the necessity of a title search (Colorado, Georgia, Hawaii, Illinois, Massachusetts, Minnesota, Nebraska, North Carolina, Ohio, South Dakota, Tennessee, Utah, Virginia, Washington give some degree of recognition to Torrens titles), secure the certificate of title registration and make provisions for transferring it at the closing.

- If the agreement for the buyer to assume the seller's mortgage is in the deed, the buyer must sign the deed. If the lender agrees to release the seller and look only to the buyer, an "attornment" form must be prepared to reflect this.
- Arrange for an official reading of the water meter.
- If the house is heated by oil, arrange for a measurement of fuel oil on hand.
- Inform the utility company of the impending change in ownership (often this will be a task the buyer's attorney will perform).
- Draft a bill of sale (if necessary) for personal property transferred with the house, indicating, for example, that the seller owns the items, has the full right to transfer them, there are no liens on the property, and the seller is not the subject of a bankruptcy petition.
- It may be necessary to draft one or more affidavits for the closing—for example, of identity (that your client is not the Stephanie Russell who filed for bankruptcy on June 4, 1985; that, although the grantee of your client's deed is Lisa Larsen, she now uses her married name of Lisa Brian), of absence of events after the title search that would alter the validity of the seller's title; of absence of building code violations or easements not mentioned in the title search.
- Inform the seller's insurance broker to write the necessary endorsements if the buyer assumes the seller's homeowner's insurance policy. Conversely, if the buyer acquires his own policy, make sure that the closing figures are not adjusted to include insurance premiums.
- Compute adjustments and prorations (for example, the buyer pays for fuel oil on hand; taxes must be prorated with regard to prepayments made by seller and the date of the closing vis-a-vis the date on which taxes fall due). Instruct your client about the amount he will receive and amounts he must pay (for example, any costs to be assumed by seller; broker's fee; satisfaction of mortgage that will not be assumed) and form of payment (for example, certified check).

CO-OP AND CONDO CLOSINGS

In most respects, co-op and condo closings are like those for conventional homes. However, conventional home and condo closings involve a transfer of real property (in the case of a condo, the individual condo unit, plus rights in the common areas); the co-op closing is a transfer of stock and assignment of rights under a proprietary lease.

If a condominium or cooperative apartment is being purchased, make sure all documents relate to the correct unit: mix-ups are especially common when a developer must arrange mass closings.

The deed, affidavit of title, and real estate transfer tax return for a condominium are similar to those for the conventional house. The condo survey, however, shows another dimension—the unit's location within the condo complex. Make certain that the deed recites the percentage of the common elements appurtenant to the unit; and be sure that your buyer client receives a copy of the management agreement and condo complex budget. Also attempt to secure the condo project's endorsement to the title insurance policy covering your client's unit.

With respect to a co-op purchase: If your buyer client is financing it, he or she executes a collateral pledge agreement with a lending institution rather than a mortgage. The appropriate title insurance policies are the American Land Title Association's leasehold and leasehold mortgagee policies or their equivalents; and the title search should include a search for judgments against the co-op seller personally, federal tax liens, UCC financing statements that could encumber the stock and lease, and liens against the co-op building.

EXAMPLE: In one co-op deal, in which I represented the buyer, the closing documents consisted of the following: assignment of proprietary lease, co-op board statement consenting to assignment, buyer acceptance of assignment and assumption of lease, original stock certificate for number of shares assigned to buyer with lease, original proprietary lease, statement by seller confirming that all charges with respect to shares (that is, maintenance charges) were paid and that the proprietary lease was in full force and effect, cancelled UCC-3 filing statements indicating that the seller's creditors no longer claimed a security interest in the lease and shares, note, loan security agreement, and recognition letter (co-op corporation "recognizing" and approving bank lien on lease and shares).

Among its provisions, the loan security agreement contained this language: "PLEDGE OF STOCK: To insure the payment of the Note, the Borrower, by this Loan Security Agreement, gives to the Lender a security interest in the share of the Corporation, represented by the Stock issued to the Borrower, together with all increases, profits, proceeds, additions and substitutions for that Stock. A security interest means that if the Borrower does not pay the Note as required the Lender may sell the stock and apply the proceeds to any sums due. If an Event of Default occurs ...and the lender demands repayment in full, the Borrower appoints the Lender as his or her proxy with full power to attend all shareholders meetings and exercise all rights of a voting shareholder of the Stock...."

CLOSING COSTS

This brings us to the transfer of the monies—obviously a crucial element of any closing. What happens quite frequently is that out of the mortgage proceeds due the buyer, the lending institution will cut checks to the seller's mortgagee (to satisfy seller's mortgage and remove it as a lien), to the broker (to satisfy seller's commitment to the broker), and to the seller (the remainder of the proceeds). The escrow holder will deliver the down payment (with or without interest) to the seller. And by certified check, the buyer will transfer to the seller monies equal to the purchase price less the mortgage proceeds and down payment.

What about the smaller items—who pays them?

Checklist:

- The buyer is usually responsible for cost of the credit report, the survey of the property, the title examination, issuance of the insurance certificate, appraisal of the property, and the loan origination fee. If the buyer acquires private mortgage insurance to permit him to make a smaller down payment, he must pay for this insurance—usually in a lump sum at the closing (unlike homeowner's insurance premiums, which are usually included in the monthly mortgage payments).

- Although the seller's attorney prepares a purchase money mortgage, the buyer usually pays for the legal work involved.

- Similarly, local custom varies as to who pays for the title examination—but the buyer always pays for title insurance for a PMM.

- Local custom often requires the seller to pay the real estate transfer taxes; the same result is reached if the contract of sale obligates the seller to give a "stamped deed."

- The costs of an escrow closing are usually split fifty-fifty between buyer and seller; the escrow company simply retains its fee from the escrow funds. However, if the contract of sale is silent and an escrow closing is not the usual local practice, the party who requests an escrow closing may have to pay for the privilege.

- No hard-and-fast rules seem to have evolved as to who pays the mortgage assumption fee or prepayment penalty.

RESPA: LOAN CLOSING

Although many of the closing costs are highly negotiable between the buyer and the seller, most buyers encounter substantial (and non-negotiable) closing costs in the form of a confusing panoply of charges assessed by lenders.

The Real Estate Settlement Procedures Act (RESPA; 12 USCS 2501 et seq.) requires lenders to make a good-faith estimate of settlement costs when a person makes a loan application (within three business days of receipt of a mailed application). Although the lender is responsible for making the disclosures, not all the costs to be disclosed are imposed by the lender. The lender must state the costs as finally determined on a Uniform Settlement Statement given to the buyer at the closing; if the buyer so requests, he must be given access to the statement one business day before the closing.

It's important to note that RESPA applies to mortgage transactions made by lending institutions—not to mortgage assumptions, novations, or sales subject to an existing mortgage.

RESPA DISCLOSURE REQUIREMENTS

The very extensive RESPA disclosures include:

- total settlement charges
- loan origination fees (lender's administrative costs for processing the loan; often expressed as a percentage of the loan)
- loan discount ("points")
- appraisal fee
- credit report fee
- lender's inspection fee (for newly constructed housing)
- mortgage insurance application fee
- assumption fee
- interest to be prepaid at closing, for the time between the closing and the first scheduled monthly payment
- mortgage insurance premiums may have to be prepaid at the closing
- the first year's homeowner's insurance premium may have to be prepaid at the closing
- funds to be kept in escrow for taxes and insurance must be disclosed. RESPA also sets limits on the maximum escrow that can be required for this purpose.
- if there is an escrow closing, a fee may have to be paid directly to the escrow agent for carrying out the take of the closing.
- fees for searching title, preparing an abstract of title, issuing a title insurance binder
- notary fees
- attorney's fees for the lender's attorney (for example, examination of the sales contract or title insurance binder)
- title insurance premiums

- real estate transfer tax stamps
- recording fees
- property survey.

HANDLING THE CLOSING MECHANICS

Once again, local customs are multifarious. The closing agent may be one or more attorneys; an escrow company; a title company; a broker; or a lender. The buyer and seller may be present, and may physically exchange documents and payments; or everything may be sent to the closing agent, who handles all the details himself. (If custom and agreement do call for the seller's presence, and the seller finds it impossible to attend, the problem can be solved by having the seller provide a power of attorney—and by telephoning the closing to verify that he is indeed alive, not under duress, and that the power of attorney is still valid.)

Even if all the documents have already been acknowledged as local law provides, it's still useful to have a notary present at the closing. Fortunately, many law office, brokerage, and lending institution employees are notaries, so it should not be difficult to find a notary if needed.

The seller surrenders the keys of the house, and physically produces the deed, the insurance policy (if it is being assumed), and the mortgage (if it is assumed) and PMM (if any). With respect to the insurance policy, the seller produces a memorandum of policy, if the insurer has the original, and a receipted bill for the premium. The buyer's lawyer gets an endorsement changing the name of the insured.

If the mortgage is assumed, the seller's attorney should send the mortgagee a copy of the deed and inform it to update its records. If the mortgagee holds escrow funds, and the buyer and seller have so agreed, the funds should be transferred to the buyer's account, based on a letter or assignment form from the seller. Otherwise, these funds should be returned to the seller. If title is transferred subject to an existing mortgage (whether there is an assumption or a wraparound), the seller may owe the buyer interest for the period between the last mortgage payment (let's say, August 1) and the closing date (August 20, for example). On the other hand, if the seller satisfies the mortgage at closing, the seller's attorney must make sure that the original mortgage and bond are returned to the seller. If the title company handles the satisfaction process, the attorney should have the documents sent back to him once the satisfaction is recorded, and should either send them to the seller or to the previous owner (if the seller assumed his predecessor's mortgage)

Usually the title company takes the deed and other instruments to be recorded (charging a fee for this service). The attorneys should remember to put their names and addresses on the documents, so that the recording agency will be able to return the documents to the attorneys, who in turn can summarize them in a closing memo and forward the actual documents to their clients for their personal files. If they did not bill their clients regularly during the preclosing period, nor were paid at the closing, they should use the sending of a copy of the closing memo to the client as an occasion to bill (or render a final bill for amounts not already paid).

ADJOURNMENTS:

The closing may have to be adjoined for various reasons: buyer's inability to get a loan commitment in time; irregularities in title; personal factors such as a death in the family. If an adjournment is required, one party should send the other (not one lawyer to the other) a letter specifying the new date and place of the closing; whether or not time is of the essence on the new date; and how the various items (taxes, insurance premiums) are to be prorated with the new closing date in mind. If the adjustments are to be made as of the original closing date, the seller is usually deemed to be entitled to interest at the state's legal contract rate on the unpaid balance—and at the mortgage rate on any sums covered by a PMM.

HOLDING OVER

As we mentioned in chapter six (see pages 65-66), the seller will sometimes seek to transfer possession after the closing. If this is agreeable to the buyer, the parties at closing should enter into a "possession agreement" so there will be no misunderstanding and subsequent litigation between them.

A standard possession agreement should contain, as a minimum, statements that: (a) hold-over seller shall deliver possession on or before a certain date; (b) all representations as to the condition of the premises are to survive the delivery of the deed and shall continue until possession passes to buyer; (c) during possession, hold-over seller shall maintain the premises in good condition and deliver them to buyer in the same physical condition they are at closing, wear and tear excepted; and (d) seller will do nothing to incumber the premises during the hold-over period.

PRACTICE TIP: *If you represent the buyer in this circumstance, it would be wise to insist on a rapidly escalating per diem charge for each day the seller holds over beyond the final transfer date stipulated by the possession agreement.*

FINAL THOUGHT

That this chapter is but a brief summary of the processes involved at a real estate closing rather than a definitive guide, and a homogenized summary at that, should be readily apparent to you. To master these processes in your particular locale, the intelligent course to take is to question other practitioners, lenders, and title company personnel. The latter two in particular are usually only too glad to convey information and render advice, because attorney referrals are a major source of new business, and you are a possible source of referrals.

COMPREHENSIVE CLOSING CHECKLIST (Adapted from ABA Section of General Practice—Real Estate Transactions Checklist)

CLOSING AND POSSESSION (Contract of Sale)

- Date in contract
- Closing and possession on same date _____
- Closing and possession not on same date
  - Attorney's fees
  - Escrow for rental: escrow agent _____
  - Formal lease
  - Insurance between closing and possession
  - Rental/lease for convenience
- Title not cleared—closing postponed
  - Duration of postponement
  - Per diem to buyer in case of default
- Closing location
  - Attorney's office
  - Broker's office
  - Mortgagee's office
  - On property
  - Recorder's office
  - Title insurance company
  - Torrens office
- At closing or possession—property to be in approximately same condition as at the time of contract
  - Debris removed
  - Broom clean

CLOSING DOCUMENTS AND ITEMS

- Deed
  - Corporation
  - General warranty
  - Limited warranty
  - Quitclaim
  - Recordable
  - Stamped
  - Trustee's
  - Other
- Affidavits
  - Survey being utilized depicts all improvements on property
  - That there are no recorded liens or encumbrances other than indicated in title evidence

•• No labor or material has been furnished within the last four months that is not fully paid for

•• Seller knows of no changes in the state of the land which would result in a change in the title evidence

•• That agreements concerning _____, _____, _____,

and _____ shall survive the closing

•• Affidavit of title, deleted and notarized

• Assignments to Buyer
  •• Existing insurance policies
  •• Existing service contracts
  •• Existing cable TV contract
  •• Existing guarantees upon roof or personal property

• Bill of Sale
  •• Signed by actual owners of personal property
  •• Shows dollar consideration
  •• Appropriate state and local transfer declarations or other application for tax stamps

• Survey: Dated _____
  •• Certified by registered land surveyor
  •• In accordance with generally accepted land survey standards
  •• Showing all improvements
  •• Setback line shown
  •• Easements shown—both recorded and visible
  •• Roads and highways shown
  •• Property lines shown
  •• Certificate runs to
  •• Property to be staked at corners
  •• No encroachments shown

• Taking subject to a lease
  •• Attornment letters to tenants including amount of security deposits and current rents
  •• Original lease—properly assigned to buyer
  •• Tenant lease
  •• Affidavit that lease is in full effect and that no right to purchase property or renew lease has been given
  •• Affidavit that security deposits are in amount of $___
  •• Affidavits that rentals are paid to date

• Items delivered at closing
  •• Affidavit of title
  •• All documents required by registrar
  •• ALTA statement
  •• Balance of purchase price. _____ Cash _____ Cashier's check _____ Certified check

PRORATIONS

- Date (used in computation)
  - Closing
  - Possession
  - Other
- Proration items and amount
  - Fuel in storage tanks
  - Garbage collection charges
  - Homeowners Association charges
  - Interest on existing mortgage indebtedness
  - Premiums $_____
  - Rent $_____
  - Service contract
  - Sewer charges
  - Water charges
  - All prorations final on _____
- Tax prorations
  - Based on last bill
  - Based on information from the assessor
  - Property improved since last bill, reproration to be required
    - * * * Time of reproration
    - * * * Escrow to be established
    - * * * Reproration by _____
  - Tax protest pending
  - Taxes cover more than property conveyed, there will be a tax division
- Items seller may pay from proceeds
  - Attorney's fees
  - Broker's commission
  - Conveyance fees
  - Existing liens and encumbrances
  - Local revenue stamps
  - Recording charge
  - Registrar of title charges
  - State revenue stamps
  - Title charges
  - Other items
- Public utility prorations
  - Date of reading _____
  - Deposit to be required

ASSUMPTION OF EXISTING MORTGAGE

- Description of existing mortgage
  - Principal balance due $_____
  - Interest rate _____
  - Final payment due _____

•• Amount of monthly payment $_____
•• Interest paid
  * * * In advance
  * * * In arrears

RELEASE/SATISFACTION OF MORTGAGE

I, _____, am the _____ of the
_____ Bank, mortgagee of a mortgage dated _____,
19____, securing a loan note of the same date. The mortgagor is
_____ and the property involved is a lot and ____ family
house/ condominium unit located at _____ in the County of
_____, block number ____, lot number ____. The mortgage
was recorded in the office of the _____ of
_____ County on _____, 19____, in Mortgage Book
number ____, page number ____.

  I hereby certify that the debt secured by the mortgage has been
satisfied, paid in full, and discharged.

  I hereby grant and reconvey without warranty the above-described
property to the mortgagor in consideration of full payment and
satisfaction of the underlying mortgage debt.

In witness to which I have signed [and sealed] this document on
_____, 19____.

Signature: _____ Acknowledgment:_____

DEED

KNOW ALL MEN BY THESE PRESENTS that I, _____
("Granter"), of _____, in the state of_____
have received $_____/One dollar and other valuable
consideration, from _____ ("Grantee(s)") of,
_____ in the state of _____. I acknowledge
receipt of this consideration.

I hereby give, grant, bargain, sell, and convey in fee simple, to the
Grantee(s), a parcel of land and dwelling house, described as follows:
_____ with all rights, easements, and appurtenances that
belong to it, to the Grantee(s) and his/her/their heirs and assigns, to have
and to hold for his/her/their use and behalf forever.

If there is more than one Grantee, they take as:

  Tenants in common

  Joint tenants with right of survivorship

  Tenants by the entirety.

For bargain-and-sale deed add,

I hereby, for myself and my heirs, executors, and administrators, transfer any and all interest I own in the parcel of land and dwelling house named above.

For quitclaim deed with covenants, add,

I hereby remise, release, and quitclaim forever the land and dwelling house described above. I hereby covenant for myself and my heirs, executors, and administrators, that the granted premises are free from any encumbrances that I made or suffered. I also covenant that I, heirs, executors, and administrators will warrant and defend the covenant to the grantee(s) and his/her/their heirs and assigns forever, against lawful claims and demands of any who asserts claims against the property purporting to derive from me.

For warranty deed, add,

I hereby covenant (for myself and my heirs, executors, and administrators) with the grantee(s), their heirs and assigns that:

- I am the lawful owner of the premises described above, in fee simple
- The premises are free from all encumbrances
- I have the legal right to sell and convey the premises
- I, my heirs, executors, and administrators warrant that we will defend the grantee(s) and his/her/their heirs against the lawful claims and demands of any person with respect to the property transferred by this deed.

In witness to which, I, _____ set my hand and seal this _____ day of _____, 19_____.

TAX ASPECTS OF HOME PURCHASES AND SALES

The sale or purchase of a home, like every other financial transaction of any size in our society, has significant tax consequences. Even if you're not a tax specialist, you should be aware of these consequences and articulate them to your client with the recommendation that he or she consult an accountant or tax planner for refined advice.

In this chapter, we will consider the most common real estate tax circumstance—a transaction involving a single-family house, condo, or co-op unit, which has never been used for business purposes.

Computing taxable profits is the first issue. The seller of a house must compute the profit on his sale. Ordinarily, any such profit would be taxed at capital gains rates in the year of sale for pre-1987 sales, or at ordinary income rates for post-1987 sales. However, the 1986 Tax Code retains two relief provisions that either limit or eliminate altogether what would otherwise be taxable income from the sale.

Code Section 1034 permits a tax-free "rollover" of gain provided that the seller purchases a more expensive home. Code Section 121 grants sellers over 55 a one-time exclusion from taxable income of up to $125,000. If the transaction is motivated by career needs, the seller, buyer, or both may also be entitled to a tax deduction for moving expenses under Code Section 217.

The effect of the 1986 Tax Code may be favorable for buyers: Sellers, unable to claim preferential capital gains rates or use income averaging on house profits that are not reinvested in more expensive housing, may respond to pressure to lower prices. Furthermore, if there is no tax advantage to "capital gains" investments, potential buyers may prefer to invest in bonds and other income-oriented investments, rather than putting their money into high-priced homes, driving prices down further.

THE SELLER'S PERSPECTIVE

Code Section 1034, which provides for the nonrecognition of certain home-sale profits, contains two related concepts: "realized gain," and "recognized gain."

If the seller of a house buys or constructs another house within two years before the sale, or buys or constructs one within two years after the sale, gain is recognized for tax purposes only to the extent that the "adjusted sale price" of the *old* house is *greater* than the cost of the new one. This "recognized gain" is a term of art (to be defined below), and is not necessarily equal to what the seller defines as profits—a distinction that you will have to explain to your seller client. In a sense, however, taxation of the gain is merely deferred, until the client stops "trading up" by buying more expensive homes. But many clients escape taxation entirely, either by continuing to purchase costlier homes each time they move, by retaining a home until death, or, if over 55 years of age, by using the Section 121 one-time exclusion of up to $125,000 in profits.

Section 1034 applies only to principal residences. Co-ops and condo units qualify if they are the principal residence of the seller or become the principal residence of the buyer: Section 1034(f); *Rev.Rul.* 64-31, 1964-1 (Part I) CB 300. These provisions can't be relied on when a person with two houses sells both and buys a principal residence, or sells a principal residence and buys both a principal residence and a vacation home with the proceeds: *Rev.Ruls.* 66-114, 1966-1 CB 181, and 77-371, 1977-2 CB 308.

Gain from the sale of the principal residence can be deferred under Section 1034 when the seller moves from what was his principal residence to what was his vacation home, which becomes his principal residence: Letter Ruling 8548027. However, buying accommodations in a "retirement home" does not count as purchase of a new principal residence: *Rev.Rul.* 60-135, 1960-1 CB 298. **PRACTICE TIP:** *Naturally, most of those who move to retirement homes are over 55, and thus qualify for the special "over-55" rules of Section 121.*

If a couple, in the course of a separation, sells a home owned by the entirety, and each buys a new home within the two-year period, each can use the Section 1034 nonrecognition provisions: Rev.Rul. 75-238, 1975-1 CB 257.

To qualify for nonrecognition of gain, the taxpayer must have a present right to occupy the newly purchased property during the two year before-and-after period (Letter Ruling 8246123), and must physically occupy the property during this period. Just moving in his or her furniture isn't enough (J.F. Bayley, *35 TC 288 (1960)). In fact, nonrecognition treatment is not available if the two year post-sale period expires when the taxpayer has placed a deposit on another house in escrow, and is suing the seller for refusal to close:* J.A. Henry, *44 TCM 844 (1982).* **PRACTICE TIP:** *Always ask your clients if they've sold another home, and when—and be especially vigilant in expediting the transaction if the Section 1034 two-year period is about to expire.*

If the seller has a house built rather than buying an existing house, construction must begin within the rollover period. The "cost" of the new house is defined as actual physical construction during the rollover period; so that if the rollover period ends in 1988, improvements made in 1989 will not be considered part of the cost of the house. For this purpose, construction is deemed to begin when the taxpayer obtains a building site, a construction loan, official approval of the plans, and a building permit: *Rev.Rul.* 68-594, 1968-2 CB 339. Nonrecognition treatment will be denied if the newly constructed house is not ready for occupancy within the two years, even if the construction contract requires completion in time: *R. Henzel* TC Memo 1965-250.

The general rule is that only one rollover is permitted during the statutory four-year period (two years before the sale, two years after). However, if the taxpayer must make multiple sales-and-purchases for work-connected reasons, and if the taxpayer qualifies for deduction of employment-related moving expenses (discussed below), multiple rollovers will be permitted. But the basis of each new home must be reduced by the gain deferred on the preceding sale: *J. Kearns,* TCM 1984-22.

What if, although the home was the principal residence of the owners, they move to a new home, and rent the old home temporarily until a sale can be arranged? A temporary rental of this type will not prevent the home from being treated as a principal residence, and the rollover provisions from being used, as long as the rules are otherwise met: Reg. Sec. 1.1034-1(c)(3); *Rev.Rul.* 59-72, 1959-1 CB 203; *Rev.Rul.* 78-146, 1978-1 CB 260; *R.G. Clapham,* 63 TC 505 (1975); *Lee Andrews,* TC Memo 1981-247; *S.B. Bolaris,* 81 TC 840 (1983), modified 776 F.2d 1428 (9th Cir. 1985). The test seems to be whether the rental was motivated by forces beyond the taxpayer's control (for example, difficulty in closing a sale transaction) rather than the taxpayer's intention to own the property as a source of rental income.

Nonrecognition is available for the house itself, and for fixtures—personal property sold with the house does not qualify, and any gain must be reported as income in the year of the sale. **PRACTICE TIP:** *If you represent the seller, be aware that the tactic of allocating between personal and real property and using a high price for the* *personal property as a way of raising the price of the house can backfire by creating an immediate tax liability.*

Computing Recognized Gain: Profits can affect a seller's tax picture in two ways: recognized gain, which may give rise to immediate tax liability, and realized gain, which does not create an immediate tax bill, but reduces the basis of the new house purchased by the taxpayer, thus creating more potentially taxable gain if and when the new home is sold.

IMPORTANT: Remember, the only amount that could be taxed in the year of the sale is recognized gain, which is defined as the excess of the adjusted sale price of the old house over the cost of the new home purchased during the two-year period.

The adjusted sale price is the price for which the house is sold, minus deductible selling expenses, minus fixing-up expenses.

By contrast, realized gain on the house is the price for which it was sold, minus the basis of the house (which can be, but is not necessarily, the cost of the house when it was purchased), and also minus the selling expenses. Because they are computed differently, recognized gain is not necessarily equal to realized gain. If the seller has realized gain that is not recognized, the seller does not have to pay taxes on the excess realized gain in the year of the sale—but realized gain that is not recognized reduces the basis of the new home that the seller purchases (Code Section 1016(a)(7)).

When a property is sold subject to a mortgage, the amount of the mortgage is considered sale proceeds, whether the buyer assumes the mortgage or the seller remains personally liable: *B.B. Crane*, 331 U.S. 1 (1947). Negotiable notes given as consideration (in this context, they would probably be a purchase money mortgage) are counted as consideration at their face value, unless it can be proved that the notes are worth less than their face value (for instance, the interest rate is below market, or they could be uncollectible): see Reg. §1.1001-1. If a note is counted at its face value, when the seller receives principal payments from the buyer, the payments not taxed as income when received—they're merely a return of principal that has already been taken into account for tax purposes.

In this context, selling expenses are the *direct* expenses of the sale, such as brokers' commissions. If the seller pays a "loan placement fee" as a condition of the buyer's getting FHA financing, the charge counts as a selling expense: *Rev.Rul.* 68-650, 1968-2 CB 78.

"Fixing-up expenses" affect the adjusted sale price and thus the recognized gain (but not the realized gain). Fixing-up expenses, as defined by Reg. §1-1034-1, must meet all four of these qualifications:

- the expenses would not otherwise be deductible—for instance, decorating expenses (normally considered mere personal expenditures) fall into this category.
- they are not capital expenditures. A capital expenditure, such as having a new porch added, would affect the basis of the property.

- the work is done during the 90-day period ending with the signing of the contract of sale for the residence (*not* the closing, or the date the new owners move in).

- the work is paid for not later than 30 days after the sale of the house.

PRACTICE TIP: If substantial "fixing-up expenses" are undertaken, remind your clients—who may feel other expenses are more pressing—to pay the bills for the work within the allowable 30 days, to nail down the price adjustment.

The costs of altering the property to make it more saleable that do not count as fixing-up expenses may be either repair costs (deductible in the year paid, or incurred by accrual-basis taxpayers) or capital expenditures affecting the basis of the property: Reg. §1.162-4.

Compliance Tips:

After these elaborate rules about the computation of taxable gains, it comes as a relief to state the extremely simple rule about computation of taxable loss: there is none. *Remember: No loss is ever recognizable on the sale of a personal residence.*

The application of §1034 is mandatory, not elective: the taxpayer, theoretically, can't choose whether to defer recognition of gain. Nor are extensions of the two-year period available, even if the delay in selling the old home is due to economic or other forces beyond the taxpayer's control: *Crocker v. Comm'r*, 571 F.2d 338 (6th Cir. 1978), and even if a good-faith effort is made to comply with the §1034 rules: *J. Henry*, T.C. Memo 1982-469; *E. Hayden, Jr.*, T.C. Memo 1983-518.

However, if the taxpayer's planning calls for recognition of gain, he can accomplish this in various ways. The simplest is to delay the sale of the home, or the purchase of the new home, beyond the two-year period. Or, he could vest title to the new house in someone else—transferring title to the old house won't accomplish this objective, because while the law requires the purchased home to be both purchased and used as a principal residence, the house that is sold merely has to be used as a principal residence.

If gain must be recognized (for example, the new house is cheaper than the adjusted price of the old one; the seller moves into an apartment, and the like), it is reported on Schedule D and supplemented with Form 2119, Statement Concerning Sale or Exchange of Principal Residence. *PRACTICE TIP: If both spouses contribute funds to the purchase of the new home and title is taken in a form different from that of the old home, recognizable gain could theoretically be generated. However, Form 2119 contains a "consent election" by both spouses to eliminate this problem.*

The simplest case occurs when the sale of the old house and purchase of replacement home occur in the same tax year (in this context, this usually means the same calendar year, because it's unlikely that any of your house-closing clients will have a fiscal year). However, if the year ends while the seller is still house-hunting, he has two choices. He can enter "none" on the line of the Schedule D for reporting gain, then notify the District Director (on Form 2119) when the new home is purchased. However, if the intended replacement does not take place, or if the new home is less expensive than the old one, an amended return will be required, and interest can be assessed on the deficiency. The other alternative, one that is far less attractive, is to pay the tax and file a refund claim or an amended return in the later year when the house has been replaced.

THE BUYER'S PERSPECTIVE

If the property is the buyer's first house, the transaction will not affect his tax return directly for the year of the purchase, though he will have to keep fairly elaborate records so that he can determine his basis in the property. *PRACTICE TIP: Remind your client of the need to keep these records, and that they must be retained as long as he owns the house, because they will affect the realized gain and the $125,000 senior-citizen exclusion when the property is eventually sold or inherited.*

Certain expenditures of the buying process become part of the buyer's cost basis for the property. Such as:

- attorneys' fees (except those that qualify for current deduction as tax advice—a deduction eliminated by the tax reform bill for 1987 and later years—or ordinary and necessary business expenses)
- appraisal fees
- title insurance

This is true even if the seller is made to pay any of these fees as a condition of the sale.

The question of "points" (charges expressed as a percentage of the amount of the mortgage loan) is a vexing one. If the buyer is required to pay points in lieu of service charges, they are not added to the cost of the property *Rev.Rul* 67-297, 1967-2 CB 87). To be deductible as interest, points must be for the use of money, not for services by the bank, title company, and the like. The normal rule would be that points would have to be deducted over the term of the loan (although they are paid when the loan is originated) as prepaid interest. However, points can be deducted in the year of payment if:

- the loan is used for or secured by purchase of a principal residence
- paying points is normal procedure in the area
- the number of points charged is not higher than local custom provides: *Rev.Rul.* 69-188, 1969-1 CB 54.

One-Time Exclusion for Senior Citizens

Code §121 allows over-55 taxpayers a one-time exclusion of gain of up to $125,000 ($62,500 for a separate return filed by a married taxpayer). This is an election—the taxpayer must choose it, and both spouses in a married couple must join in the election. The election is available in conjunction with the §1034 rollover, and can be most useful if an older taxpayer would otherwise have to recognize gain. **PRACTICE TIP:** *If your clients are in their early to mid-fifties, and are engaged in negotiations but have not yet signed a contract of sale, counsel them about the terms of §121- they might prefer to defer a change of residence until §121 is available.*

To qualify, the taxpayer must have owned and used the property as a principal residence for three out of the five years before the sale—although ownership and residence need not take place in the *same* three years. For instance, if the sale occurs in 1988, the period 1983-8 is relevant. If the taxpayer rented the property in 1983, bought it in 1984, and lived there until early 1986, he qualifies because the property was his principal residence 1983-6, and was owned 1984-8 (a three-year period in each case). The election is limited but still available if the property was used partially for business, part as a residence: §121(d)(5).

If only one spouse is over 55, the couple can still qualify provided that the house is owned either jointly, by the entirety, or as community property, and they file a joint return. However, they can't "split" the eligibility requirements—it's no good if one spouse satisfies the three-out-of-five test and the other is over 55.

There are additional, even more complex rules for widows and widowers who choose this election; see the treatment of §121 in P-H's tax looseleaf service.

The election is, indeed, a once-in-a-lifetime experience; if an over-55 taxpayer takes the election, and later wants to sell another property, it will not be available. Furthermore, both spouses must join in the election, and both are precluded from using it again, even if they divorce and remarry. However, there is no recapture if two single persons make use of the election, and later marry. **PRACTICE TIP:** *Premarital planning for older persons is difficult, and involves the rights of children and grandchildren, eligibility for Medicaid and Social Security, and many other questions—don't forget this one.*

Deduction of Moving Expenses

One of the most common motivations for moving is a new job or job transfer. The reasonable expenses of a move (including house-hunting and hotel rooms or other temporary accommodations at the new job site) can be deductible if the move is related to full-time employment at the new location (Code §217). Deductibility is conditioned on:

- Employment—it's not necessary to have a job before the move, but it is necessary to be employed for 39 out of the 52 weeks after the move—78 out of 104 weeks after the move, for self-employed persons.

- Distance—the job must be at least 35 miles from the former residence, or at least 35 miles further than the last job was from the former residence.

- Amount—the maximum deduction is $3,000; the maximum deduction for house-hunting expenses and temporary living quarters is $1,500.

PRACTICE TIP: *Remember, the taxpayer only gets "one bite of the apple": Fixing-up and home-buying expenses can't be treated both as moving expenses and adjustments to the* *basis or sale price.* Even if you don't handle your client's tax planning, remind them to discuss with their tax advisor whether it would be better to claim "overlapping" expenses as moving expenses or price adjustments.

If the taxpayer pays moving expenses, and the employer reimburses them, the expenses are deductible, but the reimbursement is taxable as ordinary income. (This is also true if the employer pays the broker's commission when an employee sells his residence, whether the employer pays the commissions directly or reimburses the employee: Letter Ruling 8522002.)

The 1987 tax reform act changed the characterization of moving expense deductions. They used to be an AGI (adjustment to gross income) deduction, and thus available whether or not the taxpayer itemized. However, the act made the deduction an itemized deduction—but then, most of your clients are probably itemizers. ***PRACTICE TIP:*** *Emphasize to your clients that they must retain credit card receipts, bills from movers, and other evidence of moving expenses.* The relevant IRS form is Form 3903, Moving Expense Adjustment (for moves into, or within, the United States). Employees who are reimbursed for these costs also need form 4782 (Employee Moving Expense Information).

PRACTICE TIP: *Sometimes the taxpayer doesn't know if he'll be able to satisfy the duration-of-employment requirements. The daring strategy is to claim the deduction, and simply include the expenses in income for the following year (or file an amended return) if the requirement isn't met. The more conservative strategy is to forego the deduction, and file an amended return or claim a refund once the requirements have been met.*

State Statute Chart

	Mortgage Statute	Opt Out of Usury Preemption	Deed Statute	Transfer Tax	Mortgage Tax	Uniform Vendor & Purch. Risk Act	Uniform Condo
ALABAMA	5-2A-7(6)		35-4-1	40-22-1	40-22-2(1)		
ALASKA	06.05207(c)		34.15.010				
ARIZONA	6-540		33-401				33-1201
ARKANSAS	67			84-4301			
CALIFORNIA	Civ 1916,5		Div §1091	Rev. & Tax §1191(a)		CIV §1662	
COLORADO		Laws 1981 HB 1178	38-30-101	39-13-102			
CONNECTICUT			47-5	12-494-504			
DELAWARE	5§932		25§121	30 §5401			
D.C.			45-501	47-901	45-921		
FLORIDA	665-0715		689.01	201.01	201.08(1)		
GEORGIA		Laws 1983 Act489	44-5-30 44-6-12	48-6-3	48-6-61		
HAWAII	402-18	Laws 1980 Act 188	502-34	247-2		508-1	
IDAHO	26-1934		55-601				
ILLINOIS	CH. 32 §794(g) Ch. 74 §4(2)		Ch. 30 §1	Ch. 120 §1001		Ch. 29 §8.1	
INDIANA	28-1-13.5-1		32-1-2-7				
IOWA	Ch. 535B	Laws 1980 HC 2492	557.1	428A.1			
KANSAS	17-5503	16-207a	58-2205		79-3102		
KENTUCKY	289.451(1)		382.020	142.050			
LOUISIANA			Civ. Art. 2234				
MAINE	532.8 732.11		33 §151	36 §4641-a			1601-101
MARYLAND	9-421		Real Property §240	Art. 81 §278A	Art. 81 §277(a)(2)		
MASSACHUSETTS	Ch. 167 §70	Ch. 231 §2	Ch. 183 §1	Ch 64D §1			
MICHIGAN	19.15(1C)		565.1	207.504		565.701	
MINNESOTA	50.15 514.02	47-203	507.24	287.4	287.05		515A.1
MISSISSIPPI	81-12-49		89-1-1	76-901	76-204		
MISSOURI		369.144(7)	442.020				448.1-100

	Mortgage Statute	Opt Out of Usury Preemption	Deed Statute	Transfer Tax	Mortgage Tax	Uniform Vendor & Purch. Risk Act	Uniform Condo
MONTANA			70-32-101				
NEBRASKA		Laws 1982 LB 623	76-104				
NEVADA	673.324		111.105	375.01		113.030	
NEW HAMPSHIRE	387:4(IV)		477§1	378-B:1			
NEW JERSEY	46:108-8		46:13-1	46:15-7			
NEW MEXICO			47-1-5				47-7A-1
NEW YORK	Banking §6-e, Gol 5-501		Real Property §240	Tax §1402	Tax §253	Gen'l Oblig. §5-1311	
NORTH CAROLINA	24-1.1A 45-80	Laws 1983 Ch. 126 §1	29-4	105-228-28		39-37	
NORTH DAKOTA	7-02-14		47-10-01				
OHIO	1151.31		5301.01	319.54			
OKLAHOMA	T6 §803		T16 §1	T68 §5106	T68 §1904	T16 §201	
OREGON			93.010			93.290	
PENNSYLVANIA	41 §301 7 §310		21 §1	72 §8101-3			68 §3101
RHODE ISLAND	19-5-13 19-9-8		39-11-1	44-25-1			34-36.1-10
SOUTH CAROLINA	34-31-90	Laws 1982 SB 798	27-7-10	12-21-380	12-21-360		
SOUTH DAKOTA	21-49-14 54-12-1	Laws 1981 HB 1091	43-25-1	43-4-21		43-26-5	
TENNESSEE			64-501	67-4-409(a)	67-4-409(b)		
TEXAS	Civ. Art. 852a 35-04 5069 §1.07		Prop §5.021				
UTAH	7-7-5.1		57-1-2				
VERMONT	9 §1256(C)		27 §305	32 §9601			
VIRGINIA	6.1-63		55-11	48.1-800	58-1-803		55-79.39
WASHINGON	33.24.190		64.04.101	82.20			
WEST VIRGINIA	7-6-5		36-1-1	11-22-1			36B-101
WISCONSIN	138.033	Laws 1981 Ch 45 §50	706.01	77.22(1)		706.12	
WYOMING	13-7-102		34-1-106				

TABLE OF CASES

The Property

Board of Managers of a Part of Peppertree Square No. 1 v. Ricketts, 701 S.W.2d 767 (Mo.App. 1985)

Dulaney Towers Maintenance Corp. v. O'Brey, 418 A.2d 1233 (Mo. App. 1980)

Laguna Royale Owners Ass'n v. Darger, 174 Cal. Rptr. 695 (App. 1981)

LeFebvre v. Ostendorf, 275 N.W.2d 154 (Wis.App. 1979)

Makeever v. Lyle, 609 P.2d 1084 (Ariz.App. 1980) 125 Az 384

Papalexiou v. Tower West Condominium, 401 A.2d 280 (N.J. Super. 1979) 167 NJ 5516

Penthouse Properties v. 1158 Fifth Avenue, 11 N.Y.S.2d 417 (1939)

Ritchey v. Villa Nueva Condominium Ass'n, 146 Cal.Rptr. 695 (App. 1978) 81 Cal.App.3d 688

Ryan v. Baptiste, 565 S.W.2d 196 (Mo.App. 1978)

Silverman v. Alcoa Plaza Ass'n, 323 N.Y.S.2d 37 (1971)

United Masonry Inc. v. Jefferson Mews, Inc., 237 S.E.2d 171 (Va. 1977) 218 Va 360

Ventura v. Hunter Barrett & Co., 552 S.W.2d 918 (Tex.Civ.App. 1977)

The Players

Arkansas Real Estate Commission v. Harrison, 585 S.W.2d 34 (Ark. 1979) 266 Ark. 339

Ball v. State Real Estate Division of the Department of Commerce, 604 P.2d 113 (Nev. 1979) 95 Nev. 917

Baron & Co. Inc. v. Bank of N.J., 504 F.Supp. 1199 (D.N.J. 1981)

Cardillo v. Cause Extension Engineering, Inc., 377 N.W.2d 412 (Mich. App. 1985) 145 Mich App 361

Conway Bogue Realty Inv. Co. V. Denver Bar Ass'n, 312 P.2d 998 (Colo. 1957) 135 Col. 398

Flammer v. Ming, 621 P.2d 1038 (Mont. 1980)

Florida Bar v. Irizarry, 268 So.2d 377 (Fla. 1972)

Global Resorts, Inc. v. Fanille Inc., 478 So. 2d 1179 (Fla.App. 1985)

Henderson v. Hassur, 225 Kan. 678, 594 P.2d 650 (1979)

Keyes Co. v. Dade County Bar Ass'n, 46 So.2d 605 (Fla. 1950)

Martineau v. Greeser, 182 N.E.2d 48 (Ohio C.P. 1962)

Miller v. Iowa State Real Estate Commission, 274 N.W.2d 288 (Iowa 1979)

Munjal v. Baird & Warner, Inc., 485 N.E.2d 855 (Ill.App. 1985) 138 Ill Ass 2d 172

New Jersey State Bar Ass'n v. N.J. Ass'n of Realtor Boards, 467 A.2d 577 (N.J. 1983) 94 NJ 540

The Broker's Agreement and Binder

American Mortgage Inv. Co. v. Harden-Stockton Co., 671 S.W.2d 268 (Mo.App. 1983)

Butler v. Paulin, 500 A.2d 257 (Me. 1985)

Cameron v. Terrell & Garrett, Inc., 618 S.W.2d 535 (Tex. 1981)

Century 21 Birdsell Realty Inc. v. Hiebel , 379 N.W. 2d 201 (Minn. App. 1985)

Colley v. Tipton, 657 S.W.2d 268 (Mo.App. 1983)

Dohner v. Bailey, 485 N.E.2d 727 (Oh.App. 1984) 200 App 3d 181

Hagar v. Mobley, 638 P.2d 127 (Wyo.Sup. 1981)

Jasen v. Baron Industries, Inc., 685 S.W.2d 330 (Tex.Civ.App. 1980)

Kruger v. Soreide, 246 N.W.2d 764 (N.Dak. 1976)

Maxey v. Quintana, 499 P. 2d 356 (N.M. App. 1972) 84 NM 38

McKay & Co. v. Garland, 701 S.W.2d 392 (Ark.App. 1986)

Menard v. Sacs, 379 N.W.2d 344 (Wis.App. 1985) 127 Wisc 2d 397

Morley v. J. Pagel Realty & Insurance, 27 Ariz.App. 62, 550 P. 2d 1104 (1976)

Phillips v. Johnson 266 Ore. 544, 514 p.2d 1337 (1973)

Philo Smith & Co. v. U.S. Life Corp., 554 F.2d 34 (2d Cir. 1977)

Reines & Co. v. Erimanga Investments, N.V., 622 F. Supp. 13 (D.D.C. 1985)

Robertson v. Humphries, 708 P.2d 1058 (Okla. 1985)

Townsend v. Doss, 618 S.W.2d 173 (Ark.App. 1981) 2 Ark App 195

Whitefield v. Haggart, 615 S.W.2d 350 (Ark. 1981) 272 Ark 433

Smith v. H.C. Baily Companies, 477 So.2d 224 (Miss. 1985)

State v. Rentex, Inc., 51 Oh. App. 2d 57, 365 N.E. 2d 1274 (1977)

UTL Corp. v. Marcus, 589 S.W.2d 782 (Tex.Civ.App. 1979)

The Contract of Sale (Parts I & II)

Bailey v. First Mortgage Corp. of Boca Raton, 478 So.2d 502 (Fla.App. 1985)

Broady v. Mitchell, 572 S.W.2d 36 (Tex.Civ.App. 1978)

Burnett v. Brito, 478 So.2d 845 (Fla.App. 1985)

Carter v. Matthews, 701 S.W.2d 374 (Ark. 1986)

RESOURCES

BOOKS

Arnold, Alvin L, James A. Douglas and Jean R. Goldman, *Real Estate Law Digest* (Revised ed.) Warren, Gorham & Lamont, Boston, Massachusetts, 1984 with 1985 supplement.

Barnett, Peter M. and Joseph A. McKenzie, *Alternative Mortgage Instruments* Warren, Gorham & Lamont, Boston, Massachusetts, 1984 with 1985 suppplement.

French, William B. and Harold F. Lusk, *Law of the Real Estate Business* (4th ed.) Richard D. Irwin, Inc., Homewood, Illinois, 1979.

Freidman, Milton R., *Contracts and Conveyances of Real Property*, Practicing Law Institute, 1975 (3rd edition).

Kratoul, Robert and Raymond J. Werner, *Modern Mortgage Law and Practice* (2d ed.) Prentice-Hall, Englewood Cliffs, New Jersey, 1981.

Leopold, Aloysius A., Gerry W. Beyer, Dorcas D. Park, 19-21 *West's Legal Forms* West Publishing Co., St. Paul, Minnesota, 1986.

Powell, Richard R. and Patrick Rohan, 6A, 7 *Powell on Real Property (Transfers of Interests)* Matthew Bender, New York, New York, 1984 with 1986 supplement.

Rohan, Patrick, 4, 5 *Real Estate Transactions (Real Estate Financing with Forms)* Matthew Bender, New York, New York, 1984 with 1985 supplement.

Articles

No by-line, "Contract and Conveyance Documents—Broker Beware," 11 *Colorado Lawyer* 2383 (September 1982).

No by-line, "Highlights of Real Estate Law and Practice," 14 *Probate and Property L.J.* 15 (Winter 1986)

J.R. Ardaugh, "Mandatory Disclosure: the Key to Residential Real Estate Brokers' Conflicting Obligations," 19 *John Marshall L. Rev.* 201 (Fall 1985).

J.A. Bauer, "New Condo Sales Contracts Reviewed," 11 *Colorado Lawyer* 79 (January 1982).

M.C. Beckley, "Compensation for an Attorney Engaged in a Real Estate Transaction," 9 *J. Legal Prof.* 151 (Ann. 1984).

S.M. Blumberg, "Risky Business: Real Estate Law Has Special Malpractice Traps, *2 Complete Lawyer* 10 (Spring 1985).

J. Bronner, "The Wraparound Mortgage: Its Structure, Uses, and Limitations," 12 *J. Real Estate Tax* 315 (Summer 1985).

J.S. Bryant, "The Enforceabililty of Liquidated Damage Clauses in Contracts to Purchase Realty," 54 *Okla. Bar J.* 547 (February 26, 1983).

D.R. Epley & J. Rabianski, "The Components of Creative Financing," 11 *Real Estate L.J.* 223 (Winter 1983).

B.H. Goldstein, "An Exclusive Listing Brokerage Agreement," 11 *Barrister* 53 (Spring 1984).

J.M. Grohman, "Has Title Insurance Changed the Attorney's Role in Real Estate Transactions?" 60 *Fla. Bar J. 47* (February, 1986).

M.A. Guralnick, "Real Estate (Why Specialize?)" 14 *Student Lawyer* 24 (November 1985).

A.S. Horn, "Representing the Buyers in a Residential Real Estate Transaction," *New Jersey Lawyer 38* (February 1982).

R.C. Howe, "Lawyers and Real Estate Appraisers: How they Can Prepare for Litigation," 21 *Trial* 54 (June 1985).

R.W. Jordan III, "Mortgage Financing in the 1980s and the Role of the Title Insurer," 10 *Va. Bar J. 6*(Spring 1984).

M.S. Levin, "Real Estate Agent Liability for Creative Financing Failures," 39 *U. Miami L. Rev.* 429 (May 1985).

B.K. Maller, "Legal Concerns in Conventional Mortgage Transactions," 13 *Real Estate L.J.* 277 (Winter 1985).

J.S. Mandel & R.B. Merrill, "Representing a Condo purchaser," 11 Colorado Lawyer 2783 (November 1982).

R. McConnell, "Protecting the Real Estate Consumer," 65 *Nebraska L. Rev.* 188 (Winter 1986).

M.R. Pasternack & A.H. Weinstein, "How to Control the Interest and Basis Problems Created by the New Types of Mortgages," 13 *Tax. for Lawyers* 282 (March-April 1985).

J.M. Pedowitz, "Title Insurance: Few People Really Understand it," 7 *Nat. LJ* 20 (February 11, 1985).

R.G. Schikora, "Prepayment Penalties after Garn-St. Germain," 1985 *Det. Coll. of Law Rev.* 835 (Fall 1985).

D.E. Schmelzer, "The Preemptions for Alternative Mortgage Transactions and Due-on-Sale Clauses in the Garn-St. Germain Act, 102 *Banking L.J.* 256 (May-June 1985).

D. Sclar, "Income Tax Treatment of Seller Financed Sale of Residence," 13 *Real Estate L.J.* 362 (Spring 1985).

J.C. Stanford, "Ethical, Statutory and Regulatory Conflicts of Interest in Real Estate Transactions," 17 *St. Mary's L.J.* 79 (Winter 1985).

S.F. Tucker, "Creative Real Estate Financing," 124 *Trusts & Estates* 44 (July 1985).

G.S.Walsh III, "A Practical Guide to Mortgage Loan Commitments," 8 *Real Estate Law J.* 195 (Winter 1980).

L.S. Whitton, "Realtor Liability for Innocent Misrepresentation and Undiscovered Defects," 20 *Valparaiso U.L. Rev.* 255 (Winter 1986).

C.A. Yzenbaard, "Drafting the Residential Contract of Sale," 9 *William Mitchell L. Rev.* 37 (Winter 1983).

L. Ziegler, "Brokers and their Commissions," 14 *Real Estate Law J.* 122 (Fall 1985).

Index